A few months after our arrival in Scranton, I finally get up the courage to ask Grandma Resuba the question that is constantly on my mind.

"Why do you hate us so much?" I say to her. "When mommy was here, you gave us milk and cookies and let us sit in your kitchen."

For the first time since we arrived, Grandma Resuba looks me full in the face. Her eyes bore into mine, blazing with hatred. She spits out her reply.

"Your mother was nothing! My son had no business marrying a woman with four kids." Her voice rises higher as she rages on. "I'll never forgive her for marrying my son. I'm glad she's dead, only now I'm stuck with you miserable brats! Every penny and minute I spend with you takes away from what I should be giving to Alice. She's my flesh and blood, and you're nothing, just like your mother was."

A Note about *Letters My Mother Never Read*

More than half a million American children are living in foster care. Some are actual orphans; children whose parents are dead. Some are in foster care for only a brief period, while a family emergency is being resolved. But the majority of foster children have living parents who cannot or will not care for them. Although they may be legally available for adoption, the chances these children will find permanent families are slim. They are considered too old; too troubled; too scarred by life to be adopted. Instead, they are passed from one foster home to another, trying never to become attached to anyone; knowing the only consistent thing in their life is that they are unwanted. At age eighteen, they are released from the foster-care system and expected to make their own way in the world. Many of them stumble and fall. A few of the strongest and bravest find a way to survive.

This is the story of one such survivor.

Letters My Mother Never Read:

AN ABANDONED CHILD'S JOURNEY

By
JERRI DIANE SUECK

TP THE TOWNSEND LIBRARY

LETTERS MY MOTHER NEVER READ:
An Abandoned Child's Journey

TP THE TOWNSEND LIBRARY

For more titles in the Townsend Library,
visit our website: **www.townsendpress.com**

Townsend Press, Inc.
439 KelleyDrive
West Berlin, New Jersey 08091
cs@townsendpress.com

ISBN-13: 978-1-59194-036-4
ISBN-10: 1-59194-036-2

Library of Congress Control Number:
2004109947

$\mathcal{T}$ABLE OF CONTENTS

Dedicated to my mother,
whose greatest presence has always been
her enormous absence.

$\mathscr{A}$CKNOWLEDGMENTS

This book would never have been possible without a large supporting cast of friends who nurtured my dreams of writing. From the first time my friend Liz told me that I should write a book until the present, I have been blessed with companions who journeyed with me at various times on this road of life.

First and foremost, I must thank Claudia Gard and her husband, Paul, who opened their hearts and homes to me. Lauren, their daughter, did some "grunt" typing work in the beginning. Claudia gave invaluable support in encouraging me to tell the story as it unfolded, and helped me to resist the temptation to delete material I thought was too personal. She constantly reminded me that the essence of the book would be altered unless I allowed the reader to glimpse what happens when a child grows up surrounded by the absence of the ordinary. For her time and energy and welcoming spirit, I am grateful.

Liz Eshelman, my Alvernia College librarian friend, always told me that I should write a book. She has been an "umbrella" who provided support and shade when I thought the book was getting too intense. She was instrumental in forming our monthly reading group, made up of Linda Fisk, Rosemary and Jon Deegan, Marilyn Seymour, and

Sylvia Kane, who cheered me on, chapter by chapter. My friend Debbie Johnson shared a writer's and mother's point of view. Thanks; talk about night-lights in the darkness!

There is Sister Lynn Michele Hartigan, an adult in my youth who became a friend for always. Thanks for the grammar checks. Jane Reiss Jacoby showed kindness to the orphaned children and still is open with her spirit of welcome. Thanks too to Sister J. Lora Dambroski, OSF, who first acknowledged the shattering of my life and chose to mother and nurture the brokenness of my soul. Thanks for the probing questions that always challenged me to grow.

Many thanks to John Langan and Judy Nadell for believing in this book. And thanks to my editor, Beth Johnson, who was able to bring into the light a story with many winding roads.

Finally, my thanks go out to my mother and God, because without their support in the darkest of times, I would never have been able to bring this book into the light of day. They have always buoyed me when tears threatened to drown me in sorrows that no child should ever know.

In the Beginning

It's November 10, 1964, and I have a fever. My body feels achy and miserable. We're at Grandma's house, set in the middle of an Indiana cornfield. My twin brothers, Tyler and Trevor, are celebrating their seventh birthdays. I manage to enjoy the party, but after it's over all I want to do is lie down in my mother's lap and rest. But Mother is leaving. She has to go clean our trailer to prepare it for the new people who will move in tomorrow. She will spend the night there and come back in the morning. I ask if I can't go with her. She hugs me and kisses the top of my head. "You sleep at Grandma's and get better, sweetie," she says. "I'll see you tomorrow."

I fall asleep early, but my rest is disturbed with feverish dreams. When I am wakened by muffled voices in the hall, I'm not sure if they are real. I leave my bed and walk in my bare feet to look out the window. It is still dark, but I can see a police car parked in the driveway. I peek out my door to see a huge man dressed in blue talking softly with Grandma. Her face is wet with tears.

I begin to go to her, but she tells me it is too early to get up, that I should go back to bed. I obey her, grateful to turn away from a scene I do not understand. I pull the covers over my head and go back to sleep.

I am eight years old. I do not know it yet, but my childhood has just ended.

•   •   •

I don't remember much about my biological father, except that he was scary to be around. Near the end of his marriage to my mother, he beat Tyler, who was just a toddler, so badly he broke his arms and legs. People told me later that he wanted my mother all to himself. I guess we four kids (along with the twins, I had an older brother, Billy) got in his way. I can't explain why he decided to become a father. What is even stranger is that when they split up, he fought our mother for custody of us. I guess he thought if she were going to leave him, he would hurt her the worst way he knew how. While the custody fight was going on, I had to stay with these people called foster parents for three months. This was a scary time, because my brother and I kept being moved around. Finally we were returned to my mother. I was happy to be back with her, but I was also constantly afraid that she would disappear. Even though she kept telling me that the custody battle was over, I was afraid to let her out of my sight.

But life got back to normal, and then something wonderful happened. My mother got married again. Her new husband, like my biological father, is in the Air Force. I love my new daddy! He is tall, handsome, and nice. He seems to love us kids as well. He went to court and adopted us, making us a real family. And now we have a beautiful baby sister, named Alice. She has blonde hair and blue eyes and is such a happy baby, always trying to follow us big kids around.

I think we have the best Daddy in the world. I had a lot of operations when I was little, because I had been born with a condition called a cleft palate. This means I had a hole in the roof of my mouth where the two sides hadn't grown together properly. Like many people with cleft palates, I had a split in my upper lip. My cleft palate makes me look different than other children. My lip is scarred where it was repaired. My nose is wide and flat, and my speech is affected, too. When I am in the hospital, Daddy sits by my bed at lunchtime and reads me stories. I feel so loved and safe in these moments.

Life isn't perfect, of course. Like most Air Force families, we have to move a lot. With each new move, I am sent to a new school. That isn't so bad. I like school, and I am a good student. The other students are the problem. They laugh at me because I can't speak clearly. With every move, I have to deal with a new group of teasing kids.

The last time we all move together is when we go to Seymour, Indiana, where my mother's family lives. This time my brothers go to one school, but I am assigned to a different one. I don't understand this new school. The other kids can't read. They stare at the wall a lot, and they can't play games. Nobody gives me homework. I realize that these children are severely handicapped.

I remember sitting outside the office, listening to the principal and my mother argue over where I belonged.

"She'll be made fun of in a regular school!" said the principal. "The other children will laugh at her!"

"Well, that's her problem, isn't it?" my mother shot back. "She'll have to learn to deal with it. I can't always be here to protect her. She wants to learn, and you can't help her here."

With that we marched out, hand-in-hand.

Next thing I knew, I was enrolled in a school that gave me homework.

Just as I am getting settled into my comfortable little-girl routine, my mother begins talking about a place called Vietnam. There is a war going on there, and my daddy has to go help fight. First, though, he needs to spend a couple of weeks in Montana. As we snuggle together in the rocking chair, Mother explains that she is going to Montana, too, to see Daddy before he leaves. Billy, Trevor, Tyler, Alice, and I will stay in Seymour with Grandma.

I ask if she will be back soon. She runs her hands though my thick, curly hair and says, "Of course. I could never, ever forget to come back to you." Looking into her warm brown eyes, I know she will keep her promise. "You'll be a good girl for Grandma, won't you?" she asks. I say that I will. She holds me close as we rock, humming a soft tune. She knows that in my third-grade class, I am learning to write letters. "Why don't you write me a letter every day while I'm gone?" she asks. "That way, I'll know everything that is happening while I'm in Montana." I tell her that is a great idea. She kisses me on the forehead and says, "That's my girl."

My brothers and I know that as a soldier's children, we have to help our country by letting Daddy go to Vietnam. But we aren't sure we like the idea of Mother going to Montana. Billy and I talk about it a lot. Billy is ten years old and the smartest person I've ever met. He knows everything about the salamanders and frogs that we catch and keep as pets. He has dark hair like mine, and he is very strong. He always beats me at arm wrestling.

I can still beat Trevor and Tyler when we wrestle. They have blonde hair and are noisy as can be. They're looking forward to their seventh birthday party, but we are all a little sad that Mother will leave for Montana the day after that. But I tell them what she has told me. She could never, ever forget to come back to us.

•   •   •

After I see the big man in blue talking with Grandma, I sleep for several more hours. Finally I wake up and get out of bed. The police car is gone from the front yard, and I wonder if I dreamed that strange episode in the dark. I wander around the house until I find my brothers and Grandma. We ask her who the man had been, and why he was wearing that funny hat with a strap that looked as if it was choking him. She explains that he was a state police officer and wore a special uniform. We ask why he had come to the house. Instead of answering, Grandma says that we should go outside to play.

I ask if I may pick some autumn flowers as a surprise for my mother. Grandma says yes.

The boys and I play hide-and-seek for a long time in the cornfield. I wonder why Mother is so late picking us up, but I'm not going to complain. She had promised that if Grandma gave her a good report, she would take us all out for ice cream. Finally Grandma calls us in for lunch. Her face is red, as though she had been crying again. I put my arm around her and ask if she is OK. She says yes, but that her heart hurts and that she needs to be quiet for a bit longer. I leave her alone for a while, but eventually wander back to ask what time Mother will be picking us up. She answers that she wants to take a walk with me.

We walk along, she holding my hand. She asks if I believe that Jesus loves everyone. I say of course; my mother always told me that. Grandma tells me that Jesus does love me and my mother too, and that he has made special plans for her. My mother has gone away forever, to live with Jesus in heaven.

I drop my flowers. I tell Grandma that she is wrong. My mother had promised she would never leave me. She was going to that place called Montana, but she would be coming back to me very soon. I explain that Jesus does not need a mother, because he already has one. Besides, Mother would not agree to live with

Jesus without me. I tell Grandma I will go sit on the front steps and wait until my mother comes to pick me up.

As I sit there, Grandma tells me again that my mother will not be coming. Something bad has happened at the trailer. She says something about a defective heater, a gas explosion, a fire. I ignore her words. I know my mother. She will not let a fire keep her from coming back for us.

It is getting dark and cold out on the steps. Grandma makes something to eat, but I am not hungry. Finally Grandma tells me that Daddy is on the phone and that he wants to talk to me. Daddy repeats what Grandma has said. He adds that Mother has gone away on a secret special mission for Jesus and will not be coming back. I tell him I don't believe him; that my mother promised me she will always come back for me.

The house becomes very busy. The phone keeps ringing and Grandma rushes to answer it, whispering so we can't hear what she is saying. People arrive at the house, including one of my mother's two sisters. I like her; she has kids I play with. Mother's other sister lives far away in Colorado, but I hear Grandma say that she is coming home as well. Everyone is either very quiet or crying. Finally I go to sleep, hoping that Mother will be there in the morning and that all the confusion will stop.

But in the morning, Mother is still not

there. Instead, my daddy's parents have arrived. This is Grandma and Grandpa Resuba, and they have brought us candy. I don't know the Resubas very well. All I remember about visiting them is sitting in their kitchen having a snack. My mother's younger sister has arrived from Colorado, too. She is my favorite aunt. She sometimes comes to help us when we move. I feel sure that she will fix everything and bring Mother back. Although she is blonde, she is a lot like my dark-haired mother.

Grandma and Grandpa Resuba leave for a hotel, taking baby Alice with them.

That night, I cry in bed because I miss my mother so much. Tomorrow, Grandma says, we will go to her funeral. My aunt crawls into my bed. She rocks and holds me, running her hands through my hair just like my mother does. "I want my mommy!" I sob. "I don't care what Jesus wants! I want her back!" She rocks and rocks me, telling me over and over that my mommy loves me.

In the morning, I put on my best dress and good shoes. We go to the funeral home, where I see a long brown box with pretty gold handles. It is closed. Everyone tells me my beautiful 31-year-old mother is in there. This is a silly thing to say, because anyone can tell my mother can't breathe inside a box. There are a lot of songs and prayers, and then we drive to a cemetery, where the long box is lowered into the ground.

As we leave the cemetery, we are told some surprising news. We aren't returning to Grandma's house in Seymour. Instead, we are driving to the bus station. We will be traveling with Grandma and Grandpa Resuba to their home in Scranton, Pennsylvania.

This news scares me very much. How will my mother ever find me if I leave Indiana? And why do the Resubas seem so angry? They are hugging and kissing Alice, but glaring at Billy, Trevor, Tyler, and me as if we have done something terrible. They keep calling us a name I don't understand. Alice is their "granddaughter," but we are "those bastards."

Once we are on the bus, Alice sits with them, but they tell us to find seats further away. I am so small I have to kneel on the seat to see out the window. A kind old black woman sits beside me and gives me half her sandwich. She asks Grandma Resuba where we are going. Grandma Resuba answers, "My son's wife died, and we're taking our granddaughter home with us. Those others are the children from her first marriage." My mother taught us that children should be seen and not heard, so I don't ask any questions. But I wonder why the Resubas are putting us into two categories. We are all brothers and sisters, but only Alice is "our granddaughter." What are we?

Everywhere the bus stops, I look desperately around for my mother. I am terrified that with every mile we travel, we are moving further and further away from her. I remember the last conversation we had about her going to Montana. Maybe I should start writing letters so that she will know what is happening to us.

$\mathscr{T}$HE COAL CELLAR

AGES 8 *to* 10

$\mathscr{D}$ear Mother,

Here in Scranton, I keep thinking that any moment you will come and take me home. It is so cold and snowy. My Grandma Resuba has told the boys and me that, since we are not her grandchildren, we will have to sleep in one bedroom. The boys share a bed, but I will sleep on the floor. We will spend our days in the coal cellar. That is where we will eat and do our homework. She says a shower will be built there, since we are not allowed to use the bathroom in the house. We must use the outhouse on the coal bank.

Except when we are sleeping, we are not permitted in the house. We may not go into the living room to watch TV. We may not eat with the family. Alice may do these things, because she is the Resubas' flesh and blood. We are not to talk to Alice.

I think about the night of the fire. I think that if only you had held your breath longer, or had fallen asleep in the living room instead of the bedroom, everything would be so different. Mostly I fantasize about being there and rescuing you. But all my imagining doesn't change things.

Who will explain to the Resubas that Billy, Trevor, Tyler,
and I are the same kids as we were when you were here?
Can't you talk to God and tell him that I need you more
than anything in the world? What is happening? In just one
week, I have become a different child in the eyes of the
Resuba family because you had to go live with Jesus. When
will you come back to wake me from this nightmare?
                                        Love,
                                        Jerri

In school today, I ask my teacher what "bastard" means. She says it is a nasty word and that
I shouldn't use it. I don't say anything, but I
wonder why Grandma Resuba thinks it is OK to
use. We hear it from her every day. In the first
few weeks after my mother died, I keep looking
around every corner, believing I might find her.
My search becomes more frantic as Grandma
Resuba became more openly hostile. She comes
up with a new rule: the boys and I have to stay
outside from the time we get up until nine
o'clock every evening. If we complain, she says,
"You bastard orphans, someday we're gonna
put you away!"

I go to the classroom dictionary and look
up "bastard," being careful not to let the
teacher see me. I have to know what this word
means, so I can stop being one.

The dictionary tells me that bastard means
"a child with no father, born to an unmarried
woman." That doesn't make sense. Isn't Daddy

our father? He said he adopted us. Maybe when a mother goes away, the family goes away, too.

The dictionary also says that bastard is a "derogatory name to call someone in a hateful manner." I don't like this at all, because it means I have to make the Resubas stop hating us. It would probably be easier for my mother to come back from heaven than to make Daddy's family like us.

Two weeks after we arrive in Scranton, Daddy comes home. His tour of Vietnam was canceled because of Mother's death. He installs a shower for us in the corner of the coal cellar. When Grandma Resuba is not listening, I whisper to him that I want to know if he is our daddy, because Grandma Resuba says we are bastards.

Daddy will not look at me as he answers. He says that things are different now that my mother is dead. He said his parents are overwhelmed by having to take care of the four of us. He says I need to understand that only Alice is his real child. It is natural, he says, that his parents love her and not us.

I listen to what he says, but I don't understand at all. I wonder why, when my mother was here, she and he could travel with the Air Force and take care of five children all by themselves; yet now that she is gone, a whole group of adults can't manage to take care of us.

I try to ask Daddy these questions. But he just says I'm too young to understand. I begin to grow angry. "Someday I'll tell my mother how mean Grandma Resuba is to us," I promise.

Daddy says, "She'll never come back. There isn't anyone to tell."

As the weeks go by, I begin to work out my own understanding of things. I decide that bastard orphans are less deserving, less human, than plain old orphans. I decide that daddies and mommies are never the same after life changes. I am still not sure who is to blame for all this. By keeping my mother, it seemed that God was messing everything up for my brothers and me. Was that what He wanted?

I learn our daily routine. When we wake in the morning, we go down two flights of steps and pass through the coal cellar to get to the outhouse, located about fifty yards away. It is a silent trip, because we are not allowed to talk inside the house. Neither are we allowed to enter or leave the house through any door but the one in the coal cellar. The door is white, unlike the rest of the house, which is yellow. It is so low that we have to duck our heads to go through it. The ordinary doors are for Grandpa and Grandma, Alice, the orthodox priest, and other people who are not bastard orphans. Then we eat our breakfast. Every day it is the same: a bowl of puffed-wheat cereal, bought in giant economy bags. We are so hungry that we usually eat the single bologna sandwich we're given for lunch before we arrive at school. When we return home after school, we huddle on the coal bank, our bodies pressed together, trying to block out the biting cold, until long after dark. Finally Grandma calls us into the coal cellar, and one by one, keeping our backs turned to the others, we take our showers. We then put on the underpants that are our only nightclothes and trudge up the cellar steps. During all this, Grandma Resuba sits at the picnic table holding a belt, in case we talk. Silently we pass through the living room, where Alice watches TV with her grandfather, and climb the steps to our bedroom. There we go to sleep covered only by a sheet—no pajamas, no blankets, no slippers, no housecoats.

Because of what we are, we don't deserve bedclothes. Neither do we deserve scarves, hats, or mittens. The cold is terrible. Many days, pain stabs through my ear as though someone were sticking me with Daddy's ice pick. My hands are like lumps of ice. Instead of keeping them in my pockets, I cup them over my ears to try to get some relief. One night, when Grandma Resuba finally calls us to the coal cellar, I tell her I have a terrible earache. "What do you expect me to do about it, you whiner?" she snaps. "It only hurts because you keep thinking about it."

I know that Grandma Resuba will never take me to a doctor, because I am not her flesh-and-blood grandchild. The problem is that even non-flesh-and-blood kids get sick and need help. I lie on the mattress, pressing my palm against my ear as hard as I can, trying to flatten out the pain. Searching desperately for a way to escape, I try to focus on a mental picture of a mountain covered with flowers. Gradually I begin to feel as if I am floating out of my body. The pain is still there, but for a little while, at least, I can imagine it is happening to someone else. It is the first time I realize I can "split away" from myself and leave this existence behind. This is a discovery I will remember.

A few months after our arrival in Scranton, I finally get up the courage to ask Grandma Resuba the question that is constantly on my mind. "Why do you hate us so much?" I say to her. "When mommy was here, you gave us milk and cookies and let us sit in your kitchen."

For the first time since we arrived, Grandma Resuba looks me full in the face. Her eyes bore into mine, blazing with hatred. She spits out her reply.

"Your mother was nothing! My son had no business marrying a woman with four kids." Her voice rises higher as she rages on. "I'll never forgive her for marrying my son. I'm glad she's dead, only now I'm stuck with you miserable brats! Every penny and minute I spend with you takes away from what I should be giving to Alice. *She's* my flesh and blood, and you're nothing, just like your mother was."

For months after this, I lie in bed at night pondering her hatred of us. I wonder what is so important about this "flesh and blood" she keeps talking about. One time, I even cut my finger and squeeze out a few drops of blood so I can study it. It looks like ordinary red blood, but there must be something about it that makes it bastard blood, not the good kind.

Daddy is hardly ever around. He spends most of his time away at the Air Force base in New Jersey. When he is home, nothing is different. He doesn't yell at us, but neither does he talk to us or defend us. I keep hoping he will make Grandma Resuba be nicer, but he doesn't. It's as though he is afraid of her, too.

Occasionally a person from the outside world shows a flicker of interest in us. The neighbors hate Grandma because of the way she stands on the front porch and screams at us, telling us how horrible we are and how no one wants us. Sometimes one of them comes outside and tells her to stop. Then Grandma Resuba turns on the neighbor, shrieking that no one has the right to interfere with her treatment of the bastards. The neighbors threaten to call the police. We wish they would, but we are getting less and less hopeful that anyone will rescue us. Our closest neighbor has a daughter my age, but Grandma Resuba says I am not allowed to play with her.

My daddy's married brother is the only family member to show us any kindness. He comes over once in a while with his wife and baby son, and if no one is looking, he slips us some candy. At Christmas, he brings us a present wrapped in bright paper. I can tell that Grandma Resuba does not like this son very much. One day, he stops in when Billy, Tyler, and I are sitting on the steps after our showers, waiting for Trevor. As always, we are wearing just our underpants. He points to me and says something that will bother me for years.

"She shouldn't be sitting with her brothers, dressed like that," he said.

Grandma Resuba snaps back, "Why not? They're all the same; she's no different than the boys. Mind your own business."

Am I just like the boys, I wonder? Grandma Resuba keeps saying so. Aren't I a real girl, then? I go over the evidence. Every Saturday, Grandma Resuba puts Alice in a beautiful dress and puts pink bows in her hair. Then they go shopping. It makes Grandma Resuba furious if she catches me watching Alice. "Stop looking at her! You're not good enough to look at my granddaughter!" she screams.

I have no beautiful dress. I have no pretty hair ornaments. In fact, no one has even helped me comb my hair since my mother died. No one takes me shopping, a thing that I know that mothers and daughters do together. And then there is my name. Grandma Resuba makes fun of it, saying that by naming me "Jerri" my mother showed she was too stupid to know if I were a girl or a boy. "Alice," on the other hand, is a beautiful girl's name.

I am becoming more and more confused about what I really am. If my mother were here, I am sure she would teach me the things I need to know in order to be a real girl. But without her, I don't know if I will ever learn. And if I don't learn them, maybe I won't ever really become a girl. I don't think I am a boy, either, even if Grandma Resuba says I am just like my brothers. Maybe I am some sort of monster—not only a bastard orphan, but some sort of not-girl, not-boy. All I know for sure is how lonely I feel. I want to curl up and hide, ashamed of all my failures.

One day, as Grandma and Grandpa Resuba stand near the top of the coal cellar steps, I hear him say that his "Black Lung check" is late. Grandma Resuba answers that after getting sick from breathing coal dust all those years, Grandpa Resuba deserves to get his check on time.

I look at the coal bin, which is ten feet from the picnic table where Trevor, Tyler, Billy, and I sit, and wonder if we will get Black Lung. I don't know what it is, but it sounds terrible. When the coal is delivered and poured down a chute into the bin, the air becomes full of thick, musty coal dust, and it is hard to breathe. The coal furnace is even closer to our picnic table, and I am always afraid the burning embers will pop out and set us on fire. Then we will burn to death, as Grandma Resuba gleefully tells us our mother did. I cough a lot in the coal cellar. That makes Grandma Resuba mad. She says I'm not allowed to cough. When she is nearby, I bury my face in my T-shirt to muffle the sound.

I wonder if Grandpa Resuba will die from Black Lung. Grandpa Resuba has lots of silver hair. He looks like I imagine Solomon in the Bible looked, but he doesn't seem too smart or good like Solomon. When a child was in danger, Solomon made a wise choice and saved it. Grandpa doesn't do anything. He just lets Grandma be mean to us, although we haven't done anything wrong that I can remember.

My daddy's youngest brother, Uncle Resuba, lives in the house. He is tall and mean and limps from a car accident. He tells us we are lucky to have two good legs. He laughs when Grandma Resuba threatens to throw us down a mine shaft, saying he'd be happy to toss us over the edge.

When he passes us sitting on the steps, he likes to kick us. He calls us names and words I've never heard before, but mostly, he ignores us.

I offer God a deal. I ask him if he can't send Mother back in exchange for all the Resubas. But nothing happens.

We are hungry all the time. Every day we have the same lunch and dinner: one bologna sandwich and one glass of milk. We are four skinny bastard orphans huddling together on the coal bank, trying to figure out what to do next.

Grandma Resuba must be a good cook. We can smell what she is preparing as we eat our sandwiches in the coal cellar. I think they must have chicken, hamburgers, and steak a lot. On holidays, the smell of roasting turkey and baking pies fills the cellar. From the coal cellar door, we can see the cars of all the relatives arriving. Their conversation and muffled laughter float down to us as we sit silently. I wonder if any of them would feel bad about eating if they knew about us.

Because Grandma Resuba doesn't hit me with the belt as often as she does the boys, Billy tells me to ask her for some hot food. When I do, she angrily tells me I should appreciate the sandwiches, because someday we'll all be put away in a place where we will be starved. I lose my temper and tell her that when my mother returns, I will tell her how mean she's been. I add that she is supposed to be nice to us, because she is our grandmother.

Grandma Resuba screams at me for a long time. She tells me my mother was a loose woman who has saddled her with four bastards. She says she wishes we were dead, and that she would kill us herself if she could get away with it. She tells me she can do anything she wants with us, including starving us to death, because nobody gives a damn about us. She says we all make her sick, especially me with my ugly face and unclear speech.

We go back out to the coal bank. Billy tells me I did a good job asking for food.

After Grandma Resuba screams at me, I want to look in a mirror to see if I am as ugly as she says. But the only mirror I know about is in the bathroom, which we aren't allowed to use. It is next door to our bedroom, and it fascinates me. When I sneak a look in it as I pass, I marvel how clean and shiny it is. It even smells clean.

Knowing that the bright clean bathroom is there makes it even more horrible to use the outhouse. The outhouse is dark even in the middle of the day, and it smells awful. At night, walking through the darkness to it is terrifying. I force myself never to need to use it then. One night, one of the twins wets the bed because he is too afraid to go out by himself in the middle of the night. As punishment, Grandma Resuba makes him walk down our street in his wet underwear. It is the middle of February and he is crying and shaking with cold. When she calls him back, she tells us that the next bastard who messes in her bed will stay outside all night, and she doesn't care if he freezes to death.

Actually we don't need to use the bathroom very often, because we get almost nothing to drink. We aren't allowed to drink from any sink in the house. We are given one cup of milk at lunch and dinner. Billy tells us to drink as much water at school as we can, so we stay healthy. He tells us that we can wake him anytime and he will walk us to the outhouse. Billy adds that we must never let Grandma Resuba see us cry.

If I never saw anyone but the Resubas, I might forget what living in a normal family is like. But sometimes I see the neighbor kids coming and going from their houses with their parents. They can use any door that they want. Sometimes they're dressed up in pretty clothes. At school, my classmates talk about their Easter baskets, Christmas presents, and birthday parties. Before we became bastard orphans, we had all those things too.

The police are at the house again. It isn't the first time. There is a nice family nearby that likes Billy, and they call the police because Billy tells them how we are being treated. I am glad that someone is trying to help us, but the police don't do anything. The first time a cop came out, he called us in from the coal bank and asked Grandma Resuba what the problem was. She told him she got stuck with these four bastards from her son's marriage, and that nosy neighbors were making trouble for her. The cop never asked us a single question. Instead, he told her he admired her for taking on such a burden. He added that if she hit us, she should make sure that she didn't leave any visible marks. Turning to us, he told us to be good and quit making trouble, because the police had more important things to handle. Grandma Resuba stood beside him, smiling. Feeling more hopeless than ever, we went back to the coal bank.

But this time the police visit is different. Billy has been caught stealing. As Grandma Resuba has cut back even more on what she feeds us, he has begun shoplifting food for us. When the police question Billy, he tells them that his sister and brothers are hungry. The police seem angry this time. They tell Grandma Resuba that they have been called too many times, and that if they have to come out again, they will press charges and take all the children. This includes Alice.

When they leave, Grandma Resuba begins screaming at Daddy that this is proof that we are no good. "Get rid of them before they contaminate Alice!" she demands. Billy feels so bad, but he was only trying to help us. I am amazed at the depth of the hate I feel coming from Grandma Resuba. I realize more clearly than ever that to her we are non-existent, non-essential, disposable. We are barely human.

We have lived with the Resubas for almost two years. During this time, my brothers and I have been isolated in a secret world. School is a place where no one yells at us, but none of us dare say anything about our lives. Everyone else in my class has parents. They bring real lunches and do not seem afraid of adults.

My teachers seem blind to the reality of our lives. When the first Mother's Day comes along after my mother's death, my third-grade teacher insists that I make a card. I tell her I don't have a mother to give it to. She tells me to give it to my grandmother or aunt. I tell her that I live with my daddy's mother, but that she doesn't like me. My teacher laughs. "Of course she likes you!" she says. "Who could resist a card from a cute eight-year-old?" So I make a Mother's Day card and take it home. When I give it to Grandma Resuba, she says, "What the hell is this?" and rips it to shreds. The next day the teacher asks if my grandmother liked my card. "I don't know," I say, because I am afraid if she knew the truth, she might agree with Grandma Resuba that no one would want a card from someone like me.

A girl named Lacey invites me to her house. I go and I cannot believe how nice her mother is. She hugs Lacey and gives us milk and cookies. I keep waiting for her to tell me to go away, but she doesn't. When Grandma Resuba finds out where I have been, she is very angry. She tells me that no other family wants me hanging around, and that I am not allowed to talk to Lacey or anyone else outside of school. My brothers should be enough company for me.

I do not go back to Lacey's house, but my visit has made me realize something. It is women that create the warmth in a home. I realize that, even if I get away from the Resubas someday, I will never have a home, because in order to do that I would have to be a girl, and then a woman. My mother knew how to have a home and fill it with warmth and love, but I will never learn those secrets now.

More and more, I drift into myself, trying to escape the pain of feeling so different and alone. I begin visualizing a wall built of cinder blocks all around me. Nobody can get through this wall to hurt me. Inside it I am safe and I don't have to feel anything. In my fifth-grade class, I have learned about the Spartans, ancient warriors who toughened themselves so that they could survive anything. My teacher said they were "stoic." I looked up stoic in the dictionary. It said, "To be tough of mind, without display of emotions."

I identify with the Spartans. I have begun to think that I am at war with Daddy's family. My only defense is to feel nothing and show no emotion. When my tenth birthday comes and goes, unnoticed, I show nothing. I almost succeed in feeling nothing.

Today I overhear Daddy and Grandma Resuba talking about where to put us. "I've had enough, and I want them gone!" she yells. "There are places for kids like them, and you'd better figure out something soon."

I ask Daddy why Grandma Resuba is so mean. He says that we don't belong in his family. Only Alice does. I ask him if my mother is coming back. I tell him that I have been praying very hard that she will, and that the Bible says if I believe with all my heart and soul and have the faith of a mustard seed, my prayer will come true.

Daddy says Mother will never come back, and that no one wants us. If I am a good girl like Alice, though, some other family might want me someday. Grandma Resuba hears us talking and shouts, "No one is ever gonna want her. Look at her! She can't even talk right!" Daddy doesn't say a word. He just goes upstairs.

Billy and I talk a lot about trying to get back to Seymour, Indiana, where our mother's family is. We know we have a grandmother and two aunts, and we are sure they would take us if they knew how we were being treated. But I don't know their telephone numbers or even their last names. One day I stop at a pay phone to look in the telephone book, but it doesn't list people by their first names. Besides, I have never learned to use the telephone. Billy and I fantasize about these relatives swooping down to rescue us. We decide that my brothers will go to Grandma and one aunt, while I will go to the other aunt. We know that no one can take all four of us at once. We divide ourselves up so no one will feel stuck with us all.

When Billy runs away, I know he is trying to get to Seymour. The police bring him back, and this time they are really angry. They tell Grandma Resuba what Billy said: that she is being cruel to us. They tell her she had better make other arrangements for us before they receive another complaint. When they leave, Grandma Resuba is angrier than I have ever seen her. She screams, "That's it! They're gone!"

Winter of 1966 comes. It is almost Christmas. I hear Daddy whispering a lot with his brother. I tell my brothers that he is up to something. We all want to run away, but we don't know where to go.

On Christmas Eve he comes home from the Air Force base and tells us he has a special surprise for us. I think maybe he has found a house for us, or that he has bought us presents, or that our mother's family in Indiana has decided they want us.

Late in the afternoon, when it is getting dark and cold, Daddy calls us and tells us we're going for a ride. We pile into the car, excitedly whispering about the surprise he might have in store. We have nothing but the clothes on our backs. When Daddy stops the car, we are in front of an imposing fortress of a building. We stare at it in confusion. Daddy explains that he cannot keep us. No one wants us. This is Our Lady of Help Orphanage, and now it is our home.

THE ORPHANAGE

AGES 10 *to* 12

Dear Mother,

It is so dark. The main entrance of the orphanage is so large that I feel like a tiny ant. There are two women called nuns talking to us. Except for their hands and faces, their entire bodies are covered. They scare me. They look like they are wearing pillboxes on their heads.

Daddy and the nuns talk about us as though we are not here. He tells them that his mother will raise his daughter Alice, and that the older boy, Billy, will go live at a different orphanage because he is already twelve years old. He explains that he had a Christmas deadline to get us out of the house, so here we are.

The nuns seem surprised to see us. They tell Daddy there are no children here now; that all of them are spending Christmas with host families. They ask if he doesn't want to take us home and bring us back in a few days, when the other children return. He says no, that it is best for everyone this way.

I wonder who this is best for, Mother. I am only ten, but the idea of being dropped off at an orphanage on

Christmas Eve does not strike me as being in the spirit of the season.

I cannot believe Daddy will just leave us here. He tells me that I will understand someday, and that if I am a good girl, everything will work out.

There is no word in the English language to describe the despair I feel tonight.

> *Love,*
> *Jerri*

Daddy says he has to take Billy to the other orphanage, then hurry home to be with Alice for Christmas. I ask if we can say goodbye to Billy. He says no, it is getting late. He walks through the lobby and out into the darkness, taking with him any sense that I ever had a father.

I bite my lip and focus on being a Spartan. I will not let anyone see my hurt. Inside, however, my heart is breaking. I know now that my mother is dead and gone. She will not return to find me here.

The nuns take my brothers by their hands. I do not let them touch me. I don't want people to touch me. They lead us upstairs to where we are to eat supper. They say that over the holidays, we can sleep together in the dorm. But when the other children return after New Year's, my brothers will go to the boys' section and I will live in the girls' section.

I tell them I cannot be separated from

Trevor and Tyler. They say it is impossible for us
to stay together; that boys and girls live in different places here. The panic and pain I feel
deep in my stomach intensifies.

This orphanage is the biggest building I
have ever seen. In the dining room, there are
fifty tables, each seating four to eight children.
The nuns tell us that all the children eat their
meals here. There is a separate dining room for
the nuns.

As the nuns lead us on a tour that night,
they show us a church on the third floor. It has
beautiful stained-glass windows. We are told we
will attend church every Sunday, and that we
will have prayers every morning. I have never
met a nun before or heard of Catholics, but at
least they do not seem cruel. Nobody has called
us bastards yet. The dorm where I will sleep has
eight beds in it. It is connected to four other
dorms. I am overwhelmed by the size and
strangeness of this place. All I can think about is
being separated from my brothers.

The nuns say we must take a bath every
night. I can't remember ever taking a bath. They
hand me pajamas, and I ask what they are for.
"You don't want to show your body, do you?"
they ask. It is clear I am supposed to understand
why. After we have eaten and bathed, we go to
bed. The nuns say they will see us in the morning and go downstairs. We are left lying in bed

wondering what will happen next, and how will we ever find Billy again. I wonder if my mother, who loved us more than anything in the world, could ever have foreseen this happening.

I have spent the last two years in isolation with my brothers, and now they are being torn away from me. Billy is gone because he is twelve. I cannot be with Trevor and Tyler because I am a girl. More than ever, I hate being a girl, because that creates one more obstacle to maintaining what little family I have.

I feel so old, and I am only ten.

The next day the nuns give us some candy with a bow on top. They apologize that there are no gifts, but they tell us Daddy didn't call ahead to warn them we were coming. I say nothing, because I did not expect anything for Christmas anyway.

To my surprise, they tell us that most of the children we will be living with are not real orphans, like us. Most of them have families who place their children here while they deal with "personal issues." Some of those children are returned to their families before long. Others are eventually adopted by people who want them.

I think about adoption. The possibility of it is dangled in front of me, like a carrot on a stick, but I think I could be adopted only if I have no needs and become the perfect girl. I do not know if I can do that.

The day I have been dreading has arrived. All the other children are returning from their holiday visits. Many of them come carrying Christmas presents they have received. I learn that if the presents came from their actual family, the children can keep them. If the gifts came from a host family, the children must donate them to charity. One of the nuns explains to me that real orphans want to share their belongings with those who are less fortunate. This makes no sense whatsoever to me. We are no one, we belong nowhere, we are not wanted by anyone. Who are these children who are less fortunate than us?

There are about sixty girls living in the ward where I stay. I have never been around so many females. I am scared, and I want them to go away. The nun who is head of the orphanage calls me over and introduces herself. She looks as if she is at least one hundred years old, but she has the kindest blue eyes. "You poor motherless thing," she says. "Maybe someone will find you a home." She seems so nice that I ask her if I can't live with my brothers. She says no, because boys at the orphanage do different things than girls do. She adds that she will make sure I see Trevor and Tyler at least once a week. I know she means well, but her words add to my growing belief that it would have been much better if I had been a boy. Because I am a girl, I must be separated from my brothers. Whatever fragile sense of family we had will surely break down, and there is no replacement family in sight.

I feel no kinship with these females around me. The first morning they are back, the nun in charge calls us to get up and kneel in the hallway for prayers. She then leaves for church, and everyone gets dressed. I am horrified to see the girls stripping off their pajamas. Their bodies look strange and lumpy to me. I shut myself in the toilet stall to get dressed.

I hate this body. I can't understand or identify with it. I have discovered the ability to push things that I can't handle into a corner of my mind where they cease to exist. That's how I have decided to deal with my body. I will cover it with long sleeves and long pants and draw no attention to it. I will not even think of it as "my" body, but just "the body." It is something I need to live, but that is all. I will not think about it or care about it. If I ignore it long enough, maybe I will become enough like my brothers that we will be allowed to live together again.

I am so afraid that someone will find out that I am not a real girl like Alice. I don't want anyone to know how messed up I am inside.

One thing I do like about this orphanage is that I get to go to church again. When my mother was alive, we were Baptists, but I haven't found any Baptists in Scranton. Now I am going to church again every Sunday, but I am not allowed to walk up and get this thing called the "bread of life." I am told I must be a Catholic to get what these other children get. I hope that my mother doesn't mind that I decide to become a Catholic. Maybe by joining the Catholics, I will find a group of people I have something in common with. Maybe a Catholic family will even adopt me. I wonder, though, if I'll be able to be with my mother in heaven if I am a Catholic and she is a Baptist. Are there different heavens for different churches?

All of us children attend the school at the orphanage. There are other day students who attend it as well. They are called "outsiders"; we are "insiders." I like school, as I always have. It is the only place in my life where I feel it doesn't matter that I am a girl. I am just a mind, and I know I have a good mind. From seven to eight o'clock every night, we return to our classrooms for study hall, where we do our homework in silence. Then we line up to take our baths. I hate bathtime, because I am terrified someone will walk in on me and tell me that the body isn't normal. So I race up the steps before anyone else and jam a chair against the door. I am done with my bath in two minutes. I put on my pajamas and hurry to my bed, where I lie tightly covered, hidden from the world. The nuns say I am the quietest child they have ever seen.

Being quiet is my protection. Since I rarely talk, never bother anyone, and avoid drawing attention to myself, I am usually left alone.

One day, my brothers and I are called to the office to meet a man called a social worker. He tells us it is his job to find us places to live. Trevor and Tyler are happy; they are sure this means they will be leaving the orphanage soon. I am less confident. I do not have a lot of faith in adults anymore. The man asks where we would like to go. I tell him about my two aunts and Grandma in Indiana. I promise him I will not be any trouble and will be really quiet. All he has to do is find my family.

Instead, he asks how we would like to go to foster homes—probably not together, but separately. He tells us that foster parents are paid to watch us, and that we could be moved from one home to another at any time. He warns us we should not get attached to any one foster family.

My brothers like this idea; they say they want a family and a mother. I ask if Daddy might ever take us back. The social worker says no. He explains that caring for us was too hard on Grandma Resuba, and that she didn't want us to have anything to do with Alice. I ask about Billy. The social worker says we will never be together again. He says I need to accept that this is just the way life is. He'll work on finding our relatives in Indiana as well as on the foster home idea.

I wonder what our mother thinks of all this.

When I get back from this meeting, the other kids tell me about foster homes. They don't say much that's good. Foster parents usually have children of their own, they tell me, and they will always favor their own kids over us. They will never buy us what we need, let alone what we want. The kids say that the thing to aim for is adoption. Adoption means that I would belong to a family forever. I'd have the same last name, and no social worker could ever drive up and take me away. Adoptive parents would protect me and not let anyone call me names.

The problem is, I am told, that most people want to adopt babies or little kids. I am already ten. Furthermore, most people want a kid who does not have any special problems or need special attention. Having a cleft palate and unclear speech puts me in the "special needs" category.

I lie in bed at night wondering if anyone could ever want to adopt someone like me. I think that Trevor and Tyler have a good chance. They are cute; they are twins; they are boys. I also wonder if by wanting to be adopted, I am betraying my mother. Although I love my mother with all my heart, my memories of her are fading. I have no pictures of her, and I have no adults in my life to talk to me about her. When she died, so many ordinary parts of my life died as well. It's those "absences of the ordinary" that define my life now. I think about some of the things I have not done since my mother's death:

- I have not gone shopping, or even entered a store.
- I have not eaten at a table with any adult.
- I have not cried, no matter how much pain I've felt.
- I have not celebrated any holidays or birthdays.
- I have not lived in a house.
- I have not been in a kitchen.
- I have not made a phone call.
- I have never felt safe.

During visiting hours at the orphanage, I stand by the big window on the second floor that overlooks the winding driveway and watch the cars arrive. Daddy comes to visit every couple of months. During the many weeks that no one arrives for me, I fantasize that my mother's family will drive up and ask me to come live with them. At other times, I imagine a famous movie actress arriving and choosing me to be her daughter.

But in my heart I know that I will be a very hard sell. I am a girl; I am not tiny and young and cute. The scar on my lip still looks ugly; my nose is still oddly flat. My speech isn't normal yet, although it is getting better. I practice hard in private, singing and reading poetry aloud, forcing myself to pronounce the words as clearly as possible.

The nuns tell me how lucky I am because Daddy, who isn't even my real father, comes to visit sometimes. One nun in particular asks why I look so sad. I tell her I miss my mother. She too tells me how lucky I am. I have a roof over my head. If God wanted me to have a mother, she adds, I would have one.

Somehow I don't feel very lucky.

Nighttime at the orphanage is the worst. Invariably, I hear children crying softly in their beds. Sometimes the little four- or five-year-old girls ask me why they can't live with their mothers. I reassure them that someday their mothers will take them home, even though I don't know if this is true.

I am so angry at the adults who use this orphanage as a drop-off place. Rather than get their own lives together, they make a decision that will affect their children's lives forever.

I get to select what I want to wear from clothing donated to the orphanage. The donations come in big black garbage bags. Usually the clothes are wrinkled and not very clean. I pick out oversize black clothes whenever possible, in order to hide the body and make myself less noticeable. The old head nun notices the way I dress and the fact that I always seem sad.

She calls me "the widow child."

Again, my brothers and I are called to meet with the social worker. Trevor and Tyler greet him as an old friend, hanging on to him, but I do not. I fear the power he has over us.

I ask him about us going to Indiana. I desperately want to live with my younger aunt, but I cannot say this aloud. If I am told outright that she doesn't want me, I don't know if I can control my emotions, and I have sworn that no one will ever see me cry. But the social worker just says that he has spoken to Daddy and that no one in Indiana is in a position to take us. They all have their own families. He adds that since I am ten years old, I should be able to understand this.

He says he is going to find a foster home for the twins, and maybe one for me. I ask why we can't stay together. He says not many foster homes will accept three children. Besides, he adds, I will soon be an adolescent, and adolescent girls are a lot of trouble.

I do not know what "adolescent" means, so I look it up in the dictionary. It says adolescence is a time of "tremendous physical growth, a difficult time in life, a period of searching for identity."

Maybe I was born an adolescent. People seem to think that I am difficult, even though I try not to bother anyone. I have no identity. I wonder if this means things will get even worse for me. I am finding it harder and harder to function normally. It is difficult for me to start a conversation with an adult, especially a woman. I want to shrink into the shadows, certain that I will only be a source of disappointment.

A strange thing has begun to happen. Every morning, I wake up with my bed completely unmade. The sheets, blankets, and pillows are on the floor, and only the bare mattress remains. I have no memory of doing any of this. I am terrified that someone else will see my bed like this before I have a chance to repair it. That would provide one more reason for an adoptive family not to want me. I begin to dread falling asleep, and I try to force myself to stay awake, sometimes sitting for hours in the lighted hallway. Once I am in bed, I will myself not to move. When that doesn't work, I tie the top sheet to both sides of the bed and wiggle myself in between the sheets. It is usually one or two o'clock before I fall asleep, and I wake up at about 5:00 a.m. Getting up before anyone else means that no one will see me dressing, or notice that my bed looks like someone attacked it. I am exhausted most of the time. Throughout the day, I fight the desire to curl up in a corner of the schoolroom with my knees tucked under me and my arms wrapped around my head.

Time passes. I am in sixth grade. The teacher puts me in the first group in math. I hear about college and how, if I am smart enough, I can go there and become anything I want. Going to college will allow me to get a good job, make a lot of money, buy what I want, and live where I want. I think college may be the route to the life I need. Maybe I will even be able to buy a mother and a family. I am driven more than ever to do well in school.

It is around this time that the body begins to change in ways that confuse and scare me. I have aches and pains that I do not understand. I retreat further and further into my baggy black clothes, so nobody notices the lumps and bulges I am developing.

I am told that there is money from the Air Force for me to get braces for my teeth. Every two weeks, a nun drives me twenty-five miles to an orthodontist in Scranton and drops me off. I go to my appointment and then walk a few blocks to where she picks me up, in front of a large department store. There is a two-hour wait between the end of my appointment and the nun's return, so I have plenty of time to kill. I develop the habit of leaning against the wall of the store and watching people, especially mothers and daughters together. I feel as though I am at a zoo, watching a different species. As I stare at these strangers, I wonder how my mother and I would interact at this stage of my life. Would she touch me, tousle my hair, take me shopping, acknowledge me in public? Would she leave me, an eleven-year-old, for hours to go to the dentist by myself?

Sometimes in the winter, when it gets dark early, I get scared that someone will kidnap me. I know I am not really worth anything, but I worry anyway.

The third anniversary of my mother's death has come and gone, and now Thanksgiving is coming. We children are called into the auditorium to be told about our holiday plans. Those who have their own families will spend Thanksgiving with them. The rest of us will be going to host families for the day. We are told how very, very lucky we are that anyone wants to take us into their homes, and we are given a long list of rules to follow. Here are a few of them:

- We must remember we are guests, not part of the family.
- We must not get attached or think we might be allowed to stay.
- We are not allowed to look in the refrigerator or ask for anything special to eat.
- We must never argue with the host family's children.
- We must not ask to use the telephone.
- We should not expect to ever see this family again, as we are never sent to

the same family for more than one holiday.

- Any gifts we receive will be donated to the poor children in Africa. The poor children in Africa are worthier than we are.

I am getting tired of being told how lucky I am.

I will not spend Thanksgiving with my brothers. They will visit a family named Smith who are interested in being their foster parents. The Smiths already have a biological son and a foster son. They do not want a girl.

Instead, I am sent to the home of a retired couple. Their grown children and grandchildren are there as well. For the first time since Mother died, I sit at a table and eat with adults, but I am too nervous to say much of anything. My hostess tells me that she and her husband have recently retired. They wanted to share their holiday with someone less fortunate, which is why I have been invited. She says she wanted her grandchildren to see how lucky they are compared to someone like me, who lives in an orphanage and has no family or friends.

I feel extremely self-conscious, like the poster child for the motherless. I remind myself that even though I am here as a warning to their grandchildren, this old couple means well. They are certainly kinder than Grandma Resuba.

After dinner, I go sleigh riding with the children, who are very nice. They ask why I am living in an orphanage. I tell them that my parents are dead, but that my mother's family might come for me. How can I tell these children that no one wants me?

Back at the orphanage, my brothers tell me what a wonderful time they had with the Smiths, who they call Mom and Dad. I am flabbergasted that they can so easily fall into the family routine. I cannot imagine calling anyone "Mom." They add that they are returning to the Smiths' house for Christmas. I know this means the Smiths are serious about taking the twins into their home.

As Christmas approaches, the nun who handles scheduling tells me I will spend this holiday with some old friends of hers. I ask about the twins. She tells me that if their Christmas visit goes well, they may have found themselves a home with the Smiths. I don't say anything; I just stare at a spot on the wall. She tells me that after this visit, maybe she will ask the Smiths to reconsider about me.

I prepare to spend Christmas with this new family, well aware that they are the nun's friends. I must be extra perfect so that they will be willing to take another child for Easter. Unlike the family I visited at Thanksgiving, this older couple is very formal. There are three or four spoons and forks at each plate. All I can do is sit stiffly at the table with my eyes downcast. I am so afraid of making a mistake that I eat barely anything. After dinner, they give me nice gifts and have friends over for coffee to show off the unfortunate orphan. By now I feel completely separated from what is going on. It is as if I am floating somewhere near the ceiling, watching someone called "me" surrounded by all these strangers. They have no clue as to who I really am or what I am thinking.

When I next see Trevor and Tyler, they jump up and down and tell me how much they love the Smiths. They tell me that maybe everything will work out, and that I will be adopted along with them. "Don't worry about being a girl," they say. "Just be like us. They'd probably like a tomboy." I tell the social worker every time I see him that the twins and I are the only family we have, and that we must not be separated. I can't let that relationship disappear. It is the only proof that my mother ever existed.

After dinner one night, a nun pulls me aside and tells me she needs to talk to me. I know I am in trouble, because otherwise I never have a conversation with an adult. Sure enough, she is very angry. "Who do you think you are, trying to butt in on your brothers' good fortune and ruin it for them?" she demands. "The boys are very lucky the Smiths are willing to take them both. You have no business trying to force your way into their home."

I feel sick inside, but she will not let me say anything. I know that she likes the twins. Everybody does. They are happy-go-lucky, open and accepting, not silent and watchful like me. I understand what she is saying. But I am only an eleven-year-old girl who sees the last remnants of her family being taken away.

The school year comes to an end, and I have done very well, as well as the best outsiders. Everyone knows that the outsiders, who have parents looking over their shoulders at home, do better than insiders, so I feel a little secret pride.

I begin hearing that the Smiths may be willing to take me on a trial basis, along with my brothers, when school starts next September. I am very excited by this idea. Instead of getting used to having no family, I seem to be having a harder time with it lately. Some of the outsiders at school tease me about being an orphan. They tell me I must have done something bad for no one to want me. If I am adopted, I will be as good as they are.

This body I hate so much is giving me trouble as well. I can't talk to anyone about the lumps growing on my chest, which make me feel more than ever like a freak. Over the last few weeks, my stomach has started to hurt. The pain is so bad I want to double over, but I show nothing. I must not draw attention to the fact there is something wrong with the body.

Worst of all, one Saturday morning in June, a few weeks before my twelfth birthday, I go into the bathroom and find blood on my underwear. Now I know for sure there is something terribly abnormal about me. I am probably dying. If the Smiths find out how sick I am, they surely won't let me come and live with my brothers. I stuff wads of toilet paper in my underpants and pray that the bleeding will stop. In a few days it does, and I am enormously relieved. The next month, however, the blood comes back, and I nearly weep with fear and frustration. I decide that the blood, like all things concerning the body, is something I will push into the corner of my mind I reserve for things I cannot deal with.

While all this is going on, I am called to the office and told that the Smiths have agreed to take me on a temporary basis, starting in September. They say they will "try me out," even though they really only want the boys.

The nun tells me that I am very lucky because I have a cleft palate and am already twelve years old. She says that very few people will take a chance on a girl like me. Once again, I am given a list of rules:

- I am not to ask for anything special.

- I am not to talk about my past. ("No one is interested in what happened to you before," says the nun. "Besides, you might ruin things for your brothers.")
- I am not to get attached to the Smiths.

I ask if they might adopt us. She says no, that they are only interested in being foster parents. Anyway, she adds, "You are too big to want to be adopted."

I do not feel too big to want to be adopted.

The nun looks at me and sighs. "You are so different from your brothers," she says. "You're a smart girl, but you never let anyone know what's going on in your head. And you never talk to anyone. Your nose is always in a book!"

How can I let anyone know what is going on in my head? My thoughts are unacceptable. I must be on guard all the time so that no one discovers what a deformed freak I am.

I go find Trevor and Tyler and tell them I am going to live with them. We are so happy, but I am filled with worries. I am going on a trial basis. I have so many secrets that must be kept inside, for fear I will be sent away. I cannot have any problems. I must practice harder in order to speak more clearly, and I hope that my face is growing more normal. I will spend two hours a day reading poetry and singing aloud to myself. It is so important that I learn to speak clearly and correctly.

If I am ever adopted, maybe I will dare to ask if I am normal. But probably not. If I am not normal, I cannot bear to be told so outright.

$\mathscr{T}$HE FIRST FOSTER HOME:
THE WRONG DECISION

AGES 12 *to* 13

$\mathscr{D}$ear Mother,

It is early in the morning. The Smiths are supposed to pick us up later today. Trevor and Tyler say they are really nice. They know, because they have spent a lot of time with them. I wonder what it will be like to live in a house again. Soon, I will go to the office to meet them. Then we will drive about forty miles from here to the town where they live. It is called Wilkes-Barre. I will write more after we arrive at the house.

Something terrible has happened. We drove to the Smiths' house. There Mrs. Smith introduced me to Chris, her biological son, and Mike, her foster son. She told me that I was to call her Mom and her husband Dad, like my brothers do. Before I realized it, these words had popped out of my mouth: "You are not my mother. I will never call you Mom."

Shocked, she slapped me hard across the face. I was stunned. She told me I am a foster child and that I am lucky to be here at all, because all she wanted was the boys. I knew immediately I had made a big mistake in coming here.

She then calmed down, telling me that as long as I never spoke to her like that again that we would get along. You see, Mother, there are words I cannot use, like "Mom" or "the body" or "the coal cellar." I cannot call her Mom, but I am not given permission to call her anything else. With her slap still ringing in my ears, I realize she has been coerced into taking me, and how much she resents me. I resolve never to be broken. I also decide that I will try to tough this out for the sake of my brothers.

I feel so torn. How can I ever be a permanent part of a family and still stay with my brothers?

Love,
Jerri

As I lie in bed the first night in the Smiths' home, I wonder what I have gotten myself into. I realize for the first time that there is a need within me that is even more important than being with the brothers I adore. That need is to be adopted; to have a mother; to belong to a family where all my secrets will be safe. Now I understand what the other kids in the orphanage meant when they said a foster home is never safe, and that I would never belong. Adoption is the only guarantee.

Today I have to go to Myers High School. It is a big place for grades seven through twelve. I am jealous of Chris, the Smiths' biological son, because he gets to go to St. Albans, the Catholic grade school. He, Mike, and I are all twelve. Trevor and Tyler are eleven.

This is a big city, and there are so many kids at this high school. I report to the office, where a woman keeps asking me where I lived last year. There are students and teachers standing all around. I whisper that I lived in an orphanage. "An orphanage?" she repeats loudly. "Don't you have a family? Where do you live now?" I reply that I live in a foster home. Then there is a big discussion about my last name, which is Zigga. "Your name isn't Smith? How come?" she demands. Again, I have to explain, with all these people staring at me, that I am a foster child.

I am told I need a document showing what my real last name is. By now I am beet red, and wish the ground would open up and swallow me up. Kids jam around me, asking, "How come you don't have a family? Are you an orphan? What happened to your parents?" I put my head down and walk away. All I want to do is be invisible and make good grades.

After school I go home. The Smiths don't get home until about 5:30, so it's just me and the boys for a while. I wish the Smiths would stay away, because I am so intimidated by them. Mrs. Smith says things to me that I don't understand at all. For instance, she tells me I should be excited about this high school, because I will meet cute boys and go to dances. I am repulsed by this idea. I don't want to meet anyone and go to dances. I have more important things on my mind, like finding a mother and a permanent home. At other times, she says things like, "When you get married and have children . . ." What is she talking about? I don't know how to get married, or where children come from. Am I going to be forced to get married?

Evenings in the Smith home are hard for me. The twins seem to know what to do in order to get along, Tyler especially. He hugs Mrs. Smith all the time and calls her Mom. She and Trevor, for some reason, do not seem to hit it off as well.

I spend almost all my time in my room, reading aloud and practicing my speech, so I will be acceptable to my family in Indiana. There is a public library nearby that I go to in order to check out books. Most of them are about adoption, saints, and biographies. As I read biographies, I feel like a spy peering into the lives of normal people. I figure if I read enough about such people, I might learn to act like they do and be normal myself.

In the meantime, it is clear that I am not very normal. Mrs. Smith gets annoyed because when we go anywhere together, I walk ahead staring at the ground. It really bothers her that I don't look at people when they speak to me. School is OK—I like English and math a lot— but I hate gym. There is a big indoor pool and the teacher insists that we get into it in order to pass her class. When I realize this means putting on a swimsuit, I freeze. I notice that a few girls get out of swimming because of health reasons, so I tell the teacher I have a big cut on my leg that is hidden by my pants. Once that is supposedly healed, I think of a new excuse every week. I have to be so careful not to let anyone see the body.

Mrs. Smith tells me she has some thinking to do about me. I know what that means. It is just a matter of time before I am asked to leave this house. I know Mrs. Smith feels stuck with me and wishes I were gone. I try to remember that she seems to really like my brothers, especially Tyler, and to appreciate that about her.

It is the summer of my thirteenth birthday. Soon I will be that thing everyone seems to think is so troublesome: a teenage girl. I get a job on a nearby farm, picking cabbages for fifty cents an hour. Most of the other workers are older teenagers. They don't laugh when I tell them I am in foster care; instead, they call me "Cinderella" and show me how to pick the cabbage without hurting myself. I like having an excuse to stay away from the house all day, and the thirty dollars a week I am paid makes me feel so rich.

The social worker is coming to visit, and he tells Mrs. Smith to make sure that I am there to see him. When we are alone, he tells me he is disappointed in Mrs. Smith's reports about me. She says I do not act like a girl, and that I am too silent and withdrawn. The social worker reminds me that at thirteen, I should be fitting in more.

What can I say to him? He doesn't have a clue what it's like to be me. It's not that I dislike Mrs. Smith. It's just that I have no energy to invest in someone who does not want to adopt me.

A few days later, Mrs. Smith calls me into her office. She says that things aren't working out well, and that it was a mistake for her husband and her to take on so many children at one time. To my surprise, she says that both Trevor and I will be leaving. With her working full-time, she says, three children are more than enough.

It is almost Christmas, 1969. The social worker tells me I will be moving in a few days, just as soon as a new home is found. He adds that he will no longer be handling my case. I'll have a female social worker from now on, because he thinks I will do better with a woman.

I beg him to get in touch with my aunt. I tell him how helpful I can be, how good my grades are, and how hard I am working on my speech. He says he will pass the word on to the next social worker, but that I shouldn't get my hopes up. I am a difficult child to place, he explains. I don't interact with other kids; I don't talk with adults. I do not express affection or emotion. Compared with my brothers, I am socially unacceptable. But he will see what he can do.

I try to make things easier for him. I say I don't even need a whole family; I would be happy to be adopted by a single woman. I have read recently that unmarried people sometimes adopt older, hard-to-place children.

He laughs at this. He says he would never consider a single woman, and that I should expect to be in foster care for a long time. He tells me, for the hundredth time, that adoption is for little children. I am too old to want to be adopted.

I do not say anything more, but he is wrong. Maybe someone who is really thirteen inside is too old to need a mother. But what about the parts inside of me that are eight, and nine, and ten? They need to be rocked and loved and nurtured as much as they ever did. Were the eight years that I had a mother supposed to be enough to prepare me for normal life? If so, why do other people have parents for so many more years?

As I wait to be moved from the Smith's home, I fantasize that the new social worker will succeed in contacting Mother's family in Indiana. I imagine my homecoming there. A big banner will be draped across the porch, welcoming me. My aunts and grandmother will hug me and tell me how they love and missed me. They will say they should have acted sooner, but now they will never let me go. I imagine my aunt running her hands though my hair, like my mother used to do. I will not tell her I do not like to be touched.

I also begin a list of things I need from my aunt or another adoptive mother. I figure this will be a good preparation for us to know each other:

- I want to be allowed to talk about my mother. For so many years, no one has spoken to me about her. I need to know that she loved me and that her existence mattered.

- I want to be able to tell about the coal cellar. Someone needs to know what happened there and how mean Grandma Resuba was to us. Maybe then she can tell me that I am a normal girl like Alice, and that Grandma Resuba was just an evil woman for the things she did to us.

- I want to talk about my confusion over my girl/boy identity. It's not that I want to be a boy; I just don't know how to be a girl. I think a mother could help me learn.

- I want to ask about the blood. It takes a lot of energy to hide the fact that this happens to me every month. I am so tired of hiding and pretending.
- I want her to take me shopping for clothes. I need her to show me how to do this thing that other people do so casually. Stores are so big and confusing, and I don't know anything about fashion or sizes. I need to know how to take care of myself in this way.
- I want her to teach me to do so many normal things, things that are so ordinary I'm embarrassed to ask anyone. Things like cooking, and fixing my hair, and table manners.
- I want her to tell me that someday I will look OK.
- I want her to understand how bad things were, and to tell me it's OK to cry.

My new social worker is picking me up tomorrow. I can't wait to hear what she has to say. The best of all my fantasies is that she will hand me a one-way ticket back to Seymour, Indiana, the last place I ever felt safe and happy. Maybe a woman will understand better my terrible need to be a permanent part of a family. I know that unless I find a place to belong, I'll never be a real girl, just a shadow person who breathes, but doesn't live or feel.

The social worker, a nice lady, picks me up exactly at 10 a.m. I am so sure that I know what she is going to tell me that I am nearly bouncing with excitement.

"Am I going home to Indiana?" I ask her.

She shakes her head. She says that she has spoken to one of my aunts in Indiana—she can't remember her name. The aunt told her that no one there can take me. They all have their own families to consider. Besides, my aunt had added, my mother spoiled me and I can be a real handful.

"What did she mean?" I asked. The social worker repeated what my aunt had told her: that once when I was six, I had refused to eat something my mother had given me. When my mother insisted, I had told her I hated her. My mother hadn't gotten upset, just saying that all kids go through difficult phases. But my aunt thought Mother was too easy on me.

I feel so bad knowing that I once told my mother I hated her. I don't remember doing that. I wonder if my mother wasn't bothered by the incident, why does her family still hold it against me?

If I could speak to my relatives, I think that they would see that I am not a handful at all. If they took me, I would be so quiet and helpful they would be glad to have me around. I ask the social worker if I can call them myself. She says no; the aunt doesn't want me to have their phone number.

My family doesn't want me.

My mother's mother and sisters don't want me.

It isn't that they don't know where I am or what's going on with me. They know.

They know, and still they don't want me.

I feel as though I've been kicked in the stomach.

Now what, I ask?

The social worker says I will be going to a new foster home. Because I am such a difficult placement, she adds, this may be my last shot at family life. The foster mother taking me really wants a baby girl, but since none is available, she will settle for me on a trial basis.

The new people are named Mr. and Mrs. Wesson, and they have four sons.

I am competing with a baby girl who didn't materialize.

Mrs. Wesson is already disappointed that I am who I am.

The social worker tells me that, with Christmas approaching and me being a teenage girl with a cleft palate, I am very, very lucky to have found anyone at all who will take me. I must try very hard to fit into this new home.

Maybe I can pretend to be everything Mrs. Wesson expects in a thirteen-year-old girl. Then once she likes me, I can tell her the truth about how much help I need. How am I ever going to pull this off: acting normal while not letting her see that I'm drowning in uncertainty?

THE SECOND FOSTER HOME

AGES 13 *to* 14

*D*ear Mother,

As we pull up the driveway of this beautiful home, the social worker again warns me that I have to be perfect, because if this placement doesn't work out, I will return to the orphanage. She reminds me again how lucky I am to be part of any family. All I can think of is, How will I ever be good enough?

The social worker adds a few more things. "Don't say anything about yourself or your background unless you are asked," she instructs me. "Mrs. Wesson knows that your mother is dead, and that's enough. People don't like to take kids who have problems, so the less you tell her, the more likely she'll be to keep you."

She rings the doorbell, and Mrs. Wesson answers the door. She is a beautiful woman with short dark hair. There are little boys running all around her. These are Robert, Anthony, and the baby twins James and John. The house is bright and spotless, the TV is on, and a Christmas tree stands in one corner. I hope she likes me.

We sit at the table and I have a glass of milk. Mrs.

Wesson says that she wasn't expecting me so soon, so she will ask Monsignor at Our Lady of the Springs Church for money to buy me gifts. Then she and the social worker go on discussing me as if I weren't there. Mrs. Wesson reminds the social worker that she really wants a baby girl, and the other woman says she is working on it. Then the two begin arguing about whose responsibility it is to take me to the orthodontist every two weeks. The social worker wants Mrs. Wesson to do it. Mrs. Wesson replies that she would take her own sons to the dentist, of course, but that the state is responsible for transporting me.

I have the feeling that both women are mad at me. Mrs. Wesson is upset that I'm not a baby, and the social worker isn't happy about having to take me to the orthodontist.

How can I become what everyone wants me to be, without losing track of who I am?

Love,
Jerri

The social worker tells Mrs. Wesson that I like school and am a reader. Mrs. Wesson then talks with me a little more. She tells me that her friend the Monsignor will let me attend the local Catholic school for free. And she confirms what the social worker told me, saying, "I don't want to hear anything about what's gone on in your life before now. The things that happened before you came to my house are irrelevant."

I don't say anything, because I can't. I realize the stupid list I made before coming here is useless.

When the social worker leaves, I can tell Mrs. Wesson is still a little hot under the collar about the orthodontist discussion. She curtly says that she needs to lay down a few "ground rules" for me.

First, since she didn't get the baby girl she wanted, I'll have to be the thirteen-year-old daughter she always imagined she would have. Next, I must always remember that her sons come first, because they are her heart and soul. Because they are her real children and I am oldest, I must always think of them first. I am never to tell other people that I am a foster child living with her.

I can tell that she is embarrassed by me, probably because of my looks. She makes fun of my clothes and tells me that Mrs. Smith must not have known much about style.

She goes on to say that when her husband is home, it is his time. He likes to spend it with his boys, who need a lot of attention. I will be expected to be quiet unless I need to ask for something. At school, I am to blend in and not do anything to embarrass her.

By now, I am burning with shame. I would like to leave the room, but I can't move. I hear her words, but I am not inside the body anymore. Instead, I watch this scene as though it were happening on TV. As she continues, telling me how I might look OK if it weren't for my teeth and the scar on my lip, I move further and further from her in my mind.

Finally she stops talking, but not before she asks why I don't look at her while she speaks. I can't answer her, because I'm not allowed to tell her anything about my life before today. I just shrug my shoulders and slump lower in the kitchen chair. She says that I may go to my room, but that I am to remember that I am only here on a trial basis. If I don't work out, she can get another foster kid.

Today I started school at Our Lady of the Springs. Christmas is only two weeks away, and the eighth-grade class I am placed in is getting ready for the annual Christmas pageant. My teacher is a nun named Sister Margo. She is dressed all in blue and seems kind. Before she introduces me, I ask if I can use "Wesson" as my last name, so the kids won't know that I'm in foster care. She says that is up to Mrs. Wesson, who is standing in the hallway. As Sister Margo leaves to speak with her, I notice each girl in the classroom is wearing a uniform just like the one I have. I am glad that what I wear is finally OK. At least in that way, I will blend in.

Sister Margo returns and whispers that Mrs. Wesson doesn't want me to use her family's name, because I am here only on a trial basis. She doesn't want to give the impression that our relationship is permanent. The nun asks if I understand. I nod my head "yes," but my heart says "no."

When I get home today, Mrs. Wesson tells me that every two weeks, the social worker will be picking me up from work to go to the ortho-dontist. She repeats that I need to understand that while she is getting paid to keep me, having to drive me from Clark Summit to Scranton twice a month is a bit much to ask. When I am married and have children, she adds, I will understand that my own children always come first.

I have my doubts about that. I don't think I'll ever understand. I would rather die than treat any child the way I am treated.

At Christmas, Mrs. Wesson hands me some gifts. She tells me that I have to thank the priest from Our Lady of the Springs Church. As I arrived so unexpectedly, she asked the priest, who is a close friend, for the money.

Why did Mrs. Wesson have to tell me the priest gave her the money? Couldn't she let me think she and her husband bought me the gifts? It's not that Christmas means much to me. It's just that it's hard to be this close to a real fami-ly, but left standing at the back door, waiting to be invited in. I find myself watching Mrs. Wesson when she isn't looking because I find women so fascinating and intimidating. How do they know how to be mothers? Mrs. Wesson is always touching her sons. She hugs them, tousles their hair, and pats their heads as she walks by. I wish she would brush the hair off my face or hug me, but I am too different for that to ever happen.

Today, Mrs. Wesson weighs me on the bathroom scale. I weigh 120 pounds. "That's too much for any thirteen-year-old girl to weigh," she says. "Overweight people are disgusting and lazy. We're going to have to cut back on your food and get that weight off." I am willing to do whatever she wants, because I figure she is my last chance to have a mother. Even though I don't feel heavy, maybe she will like me better if I am thinner. I know she doesn't like me much yet. At night, when Mr. Wesson is late getting home, I hear her on the phone with her friend Marie, complaining about being stuck with me. She tells the social worker that I sit in a tree with my nose in a book instead of interacting with people. I don't look others in the eye and I walk around staring at the ground. The social worker reminds me that I'd better start acting more normal, or I'll be sent away again.

Today the social worker picked me up from school for my orthodontist appointment. All the other kids stared at her, asking who she was and why she was here. I tell them. Another girl says that her mother takes her to appointments like that, and the other kids nod in agreement. I say that when you are a foster child, a thousand people take you a thousand places, so you never get comfortable being anywhere. One kid asks if being a foster kid means I never stay long in one place. I say that's right, that I could go home today and learn I was moving with no notice.

It's funny, but after that the kids act a little different towards me. Some tell me they feel bad, and that they can't imagine not having a mother. One girl who had teased me about being a foster kid apologizes, and says she will stop it.

Maybe I didn't get anywhere in my search for a family, but I feel less alone today. I hope my mother in heaven thinks I did OK.

It's time for parent-teacher conferences at school. Mrs. Wesson says she will try to see my teacher, but only if she has time after seeing her own sons' teachers. I want her to talk to Sister Margo, because I know that even if I am ugly and boyish and withdrawn, Sister Margo will tell her I am a good student. Sister Margo tells me I am smart and will do well in college someday. I always tell her I am going to college so that I can become a real person. She laughs good-naturedly and says I'm already a real person. She just doesn't know the reality of my world, or that no one really believes I'll ever amount to anything. Sister Margo does talk to Mrs. Wesson and tells her I'm a good student. Mrs. Wesson tells me not to think too well of myself, because I'm still so different than other girls. I block out what she says. Someday I will be somebody.

Robert, Mrs. Wesson's oldest son, ran away after school today. He is three years younger than I am, and for a little kid he's all right. I don't know why he ran away. I do know that his mother has been very moody lately. I feel as though I am walking on eggshells around her, trying not to do anything that will set off her anger. I know there have been muffled discussions of Mr. Wesson and a job transfer. Maybe Robert has been getting some share of Mrs. Wesson's bad mood, and that's why he's run away. Anyway, he's gone, it's 9:30 at night, and Mrs. Wesson is crying hysterically. She tells me to get in the car and we go driving off to search for him. Between sobs, Mrs. Wesson tells me that someday, when I have kids of my own (why does everyone assume I am going to have children?) I will understand how much this upsets her. Until I have my own real flesh and blood children, she tells me, I will never understand. She adds that while it is nothing personal, she could never love me as she loves her sons.

I slink down further in the front seat, wondering why people always say "It's nothing personal" before they tell you incredibly hurtful personal things.

When we get home, Robert is there with his

dad. He'd gotten into a fight at school and was scared he'd be in trouble when he got home. Mrs. Wesson cries some more and hugs him.

Mother's Day is coming, and Robert is busy planning a surprise for his mom. I ask him how he celebrates the day. He says he gets to thank her for always being there for him, and that she makes a big fuss over any little gift or card he gives her. He tells me I should give her a card too, and offers to buy one for me.

I think about what kind of gift I could give her. I know it annoys her that I don't call her anything: not Mrs. Wesson, not "Mom," not "Mother." So in the card, I ask her if I can call her "Mom." She reads the card and says, "If you want to, OK, but just remember I'm not really your mother. You don't have to give me Mother's Day cards." She gives the card back to me. When I am back in my room, I rip it up. I feel so stupid.

A girl in my class invites me to her birthday party. I am so surprised and pleased. Mrs. Wesson says I can go if I can find a ride. Fortunately another girl who is going lives in our development, and she says her mother will take me. I'm beginning to think some of the other kids actually like me, even if Mrs. Wesson thinks I am so different than them.

The party is fabulous. The girl's house is a big old stone building, with a large back deck and land as far as I can see. Her mother has placed things called favors at every child's place. Her father is walking around snapping pictures, while someone cooks hot dogs and hamburgers on a big outdoor grill. The birthday girl's mother introduces herself. She tells me her daughter has said I am new to the school this year, and staying in a foster home. I grow beet red and steel myself against whatever she might say next. But she goes on to say it is good to meet me, and that she's heard how nice and smart I am. She tells me that when her daughter learned I was in foster care, she came home and hugged her, saying she felt so lucky to have a mother. The mother thanked me for helping her daughter appreciate what she has. Then she wished me good luck finding a permanent home, and hoped I would enjoy the party.

This conversation was the nicest one I can remember having with an adult since my mother died. It made me feel good to think that somehow, I've made a positive difference in this family's life. It gave me such a boost of confidence that I decide to bring my desire to be adopted out in the open. I will tell Mrs. Wesson directly how much I want to be part of her family. I am extra careful in my behavior as I wait for the right moment. I do not ask for anything or draw any attention to myself. I block out anything that Mrs. Wesson says about the body or how it is too fat. I focus intently on the cherished prize: adoption. If I am adopted, Mrs. Wesson will have to love and mother me. The law says that adopted children are the same as biological children.

Mrs. Wesson is in the kitchen when I approach her and ask if we can talk. She says that I must make it quick, as she has somewhere to go. I blurt out how much I want to be part of the family and have a permanent mother. I say I want most of all to be adopted by her and her husband. I point out how much my speech has improved, and that my grades are good. I also tell her I know I'm not the normal girl she wanted for a daughter, but if she will adopt me I will try my best to be perfect. I'll try to make all my faults go away.

She stops me in the middle of my pleading and tells me to go outside, because she has to talk with her husband. She says that there are a lot of changes coming in their lives, and she doesn't know if I can fit into their plans.

I go outside feeling crushed, but unable to give up the hope that burns within me. I have so few options for gaining a family and becoming a girl, a woman, a human being.

After a few minutes, the Wessons call me back to the kitchen and tell me to sit down. Mrs. Wesson tells me that the answer is no.

Mr. Wesson, sensing my disappointment,

quickly adds that he has encouraged his wife to keep working with me, especially since he is being transferred from Pennsylvania to Wichita, Kansas. He says that his wife is going to be under a lot of stress, because he'll be away in Kansas for weeks, getting started with his job and looking for a new house. If I am very helpful with the boys and make Mrs. Wesson's life easier, he says, they might reconsider adopting me.

I hear myself saying that I will do anything to be helpful to Mrs. Wesson. I will turn myself inside out if it means I can fit in well enough to be adopted. But as I am talking, another part of me is watching Mrs. Wesson, and I know she is not happy. She is angry about the job transfer and the fact that Mr. Wesson will be gone so much. I'm not happy about that, either. When Mr. Wesson is around, Mrs. Wesson is not nearly so short-tempered or caustic in her remarks to me.

Eighth-grade graduation is next week. I have done very well. School is really cool sometimes, because the battle to pass or fail is completely up to me. It's not like trying to become a normal human or girl, a process that depends upon a thousand nuances, all involving other people. I understand the rules of getting good grades. I can grow my brain power, increase my vocabulary, understand mathematical concepts, and explore scientific experiments. I can succeed in final exams in school, unlike those I have to take in real life. I seem doomed to fail life exams, which involve emotions, acceptance, and having an identity. I comfort myself with the idea that given all I have been through since my mother died, any success, even if it's only passing a school exam, is really an accomplishment. It's sad that I'm the only one who seems to believe that. No one else believes I can do anything.

Mrs. Wesson says she is embarrassed to be seen with me at the graduation ceremony because I am so fat. The priest has given her money to buy me a dress. She doesn't want me to go shopping with her for it; she says she'll pick one out. I suppose she doesn't want to be seen in public with me. Maybe when she sees me graduate, she will feel differently about me. Maybe being smart will make up for the aspects of me that she finds so despicable.

Sister Margo wishes me good luck as I leave her class. She tells me to keep setting goals and not to let anyone discourage me. I like Sister Margo. I tell her how much I hate being a foster child and how much I want to be adopted, even if I am too old to need a mother. She laughs in her gentle way and tells me that every child, even a thirteen-year-old like me, needs a mother and deserves to have one. She doesn't seem to think I'm so strange—just a kid trying to find her way in life.

Mr. and Mrs. Wesson do come to the graduation mass, but they sit way in the back of the auditorium. I still am not allowed to use their name, but I feel sure that someday I'll have a different one. When I am handed my diploma, I feel wonderful. I just wish I knew what came next! I hope my mother in heaven is proud of me because of my good grades.

The day after graduation, I again approach Mrs. Wesson to talk about adoption. In school I have learned the rules for debating an issue, and I know I must present my side of the argument effectively. I make two lists, comparing adoption and foster care:

Adoption of Me

1. I'll be permanent, never moved.
2. I'll have the same last name as my family.
3. I'll be a real person.
4. I'll get a job and give my family money.
5. My family won't have to give me anything.
6. I'll have what I want most: a mother.

Me Being a Foster Kid

1. I'll always be shuffled around.
2. I'll have to carry the name of a family that despises my existence.
3. I'll never be a real person, girl, daughter, or woman.
4. People have to be paid to keep me.
5. I don't get anything.
6. I'll never be loved or nurtured, mothered or touched.

When I approach Mrs. Wesson, I decide not to mention the foster kid list, because I'm afraid she will like that side of the argument better. Instead, I tell her I have been doing some research and believe that if she and Mr. Wesson adopt me, I'll be able to help support the family. I tell her I think I can will myself into becoming whatever kind of daughter she wants.

Mrs. Wesson answers that it will be months before they think about adoption. She tells me that the social worker will be coming tomorrow to give the OK for me to go with them to Wichita. I nod, but my heart sinks. I obviously don't know how to sell myself effectively.

When the social worker comes, she asks if I want to go to Kansas. I say yes, because I figure the longer I stay with the Wessons, the more likely they are to get attached to me and adopt me. The social worker says that the Wessons have never mentioned adoption, but that she will give her permission for me to go along as a foster child. I thank her, but I add that I will not always be a foster child, being shuffled around like this. I am going to belong permanently someday. She says that I have a stubborn streak and that I should learn to accept reality.

What reality does she want me to accept? That I am nothing? That I am so repulsive that no one will ever adopt me? That my hunger to be mothered is so terribly wrong? But I just tell her that I will be good and helpful. She wishes me luck and says that if things don't work out, I will be returned to the orphanage.

To my surprise, Mrs. Wesson says that Daddy will come to see me today. I have not seen him in two years, but he is still legally responsible for me, and he needs to give his permission for me to leave the state. Our meeting is brief. I feel a wisp of nostalgia when I see him, remembering when he and my mother and brothers and I were all together. But I quickly brush those old memories away. He asks if I want to go to Kansas. I tell him yes, and for the first time I tell him how badly I want to be adopted and have a mother. I say that I think my mother would understand. He reminds me that if I am adopted, I will have to change my last name. I want to laugh that he thinks this would be a problem for me. Why would I want to keep a name that is a daily reminder of how despicable I am? But I keep silent. What's the point of getting into an argument with this stranger, a person who abandoned me so long ago? Someday, I really believe that Daddy will have to answer to my mother and God, not so much for what he did, but for what he failed to do. He didn't protect us, he didn't love us, and mostly, he allowed his parents to continue playing out their hatred of our mother through their neglect and abuse of us.

The really sad part is that I loved him. We have been severed in a way that no amount of forgiveness can ever heal. I still remember how my brothers and I tagged after him everywhere when my mother was still part of our lives. How could he have so dishonored my mother by turning his back on us?

As we prepare for the move, Mrs. Wesson begins making me more nervous than ever. She has always been somewhat moody, but now her emotional swings are becoming more extreme. The slightest thing can set her off and unleash acid-laced remarks. As much as possible I try to fade into the woodwork, hoping not to be the target of her anger. I am told that we will be going to St. Louis for a few weeks, where we will stay with Mrs. Wesson's mother. During this time, Mr. and Mrs. Wesson will go to Wichita and start looking for a house. While we are packing, Mrs. Wesson warns me that I had better not cause any problems at her mother's house, and calls me an added inconvenience. I sense that Mrs. Wesson is not happy about going to her mother's house, but this house has been sold, and we have to get out. I promise her that she won't even know that I am around, and that I will take the twins, James and John, out every day.

Living with someone who has severe mood swings is like living in a funhouse filled with mirrors—except that it's not fun. I am constantly trying to find my way from room to room and crashing into a mirror. It's impossible to know where one mood ends and the next begins. I am increasingly feeling the heat of Mrs. Wesson's anger, even though the things she seems angriest about have nothing to do with me.

Now we are in St. Louis. Mrs. Wesson tells me that I am not to speak unless I am spoken to, and that I must remember her mother is the boys' grandmother first. Every morning after she gets the twins dressed and fed, I am to take them in their stroller to a nearby park. At 11:30 a.m. I bring them home to her. She meets us at the door and tells me to go away again until five or six o'clock. I am not invited in for lunch. I wonder what is going on, why I can't eat lunch with the boys, but no one explains.

So I return to the park day after day and sit on the swing there. A mobile library stops at the park, so I check out some poetry books and work on my speech. How will I ever learn more about living in a family if I am always by myself?

Now Mrs. Wesson is furious at me. I sleep in the same room as James and John. There are two twin beds there. I sleep in one, and the twins share the other. They have always slept in a crib before. One night, James cries nearly all night. When I tell Mrs. Wesson this, she starts screaming that I must have done something to him. I swear to her that I didn't; he's just afraid of the big bed and that it is so dark in the room. But she tells me to shut up and not to try to defend myself. "I was crazy to listen to my husband and bring you along here!" she yells. "If James cries again tonight, I'm putting you on the first plane back to the orphanage."

When night comes and James begins to cry, I take him into my bed and rock him until he falls asleep. It's so strange that Mrs. Wesson thinks I hurt James, yet she continues to make me sleep in the room with the twins. If I had kids and I thought someone had hurt them, I would never let that person near them again.

I tell Mrs. Wesson that James didn't cry last night. She tells me not to speak to her. I ask what I've done wrong. She refuses to answer.

I eat my breakfast quickly, trying to figure out what I've done to upset her now. As she dresses James and John, she tells Robert to tell me, even though I'm standing right there, to come back after lunch to take the twins out again for the whole afternoon.

I groan inwardly, but I don't say anything. I wonder if she knows how much work it is to keep two baby boys entertained all morning. And now I have to do it all afternoon as well. Plus, it's so hot outside. Robert and Anthony get to hang around the cool house. It doesn't seem fair.

From overhearing the conversation around me, I learn that Mrs. Wesson is flying to Kansas to check out a house they might buy. Her mother is older and doesn't want to have total care of the boys. Maybe I am not being as helpful as I said I'd be. I accept the idea that I will take them to the park for the whole day, except for the two hours that I bring them home to eat lunch and get changed.

During their lunchtime, I sit on the steps outside. I am not offered any food.

While Mrs. Wesson is in Kansas, I take care of James and John for most of the day. The social worker telephones to see how I am. After all the rides to the orthodontist over the past six months, I grew to sort of like her. Sometimes I secretly wish that social workers could adopt kids like me. They seem to understand that we are not so strange. During our talk, the social worker asks what I do during the day, so I tell her. She seems disturbed. She says she doesn't like the idea of a thirteen-year-old having the responsibility of watching two babies all day. She says she'll talk to Mrs. Wesson about using me as a full-time babysitter. I beg her not to say anything, because I don't need Mrs. Wesson having any more excuses to be angry at me. The social worker tells me not to worry about anything.

Mrs. Wesson comes back to St. Louis and says we will be moving in two weeks. She calls the social worker, and when she hangs up she is livid with me. "How dare you complain about anything!" she screams. She announces that from now on, she will watch her own children. As for me, I am to leave the house after breakfast and not come back until dinnertime. So I spend my days walking the streets of St. Louis, as though I'm wandering through an unknown planet. My sense of isolation is overpowering.

We fly to Wichita, where Mr. Wesson is waiting for us. Ever since the conversation with the social worker, Mrs. Wesson will not speak to me. If she has anything to say, she tells Robert to tell me. The punishing silence is excruciating, especially because I don't know what I'm being punished for. At mass on Sundays, I sit in the back of the church while the Wessons sit together in front. I know Mrs. Wesson would be humiliated if anyone knew we were together.

The new house is a townhouse, and it is beautiful. When I am grown up I would like to have my own house, only it would be a log cabin like Davy Crockett's. The only thing I don't like about the house is that I have to sleep in the basement with the twins on a big pull-out couch. The basement is so big and dark at night. It is nothing like the Resuba's coal cellar, but being in the basement tells me something about my symbolic place in this family. James and John are good babies, and I often rock James to sleep, but I'm always afraid they might fall off the couch and that I will be blamed. I stay awake much of the night to see that nothing happens to them.

I hear Mrs. Wesson on the phone a lot with her friend back in Pennsylvania. She complains that nothing is going right. Mr. Wesson is never home; there is so much work to do; and the last thing she needs is this foster kid. She says she wants to send me back, because I am nothing like the daughter she imagined. I sit on the basement stairs listening to this, trying desperately to stem the tide of tears that threatens to overwhelm me. I'm trying so hard to be what she wants, but I can't figure out how.

It is my fourteenth birthday today. No one acknowledges it. When I come up from the basement, I hear Mrs. Wesson having a lively conversation with the boys. When I pass the kitchen door, she becomes silent. I have no breakfast, because there is no place set for me. I ask if I can have something to eat. Mrs. Wesson tells Robert to tell me that I should leave the house. I may stop back in the afternoon, when I will find something on the table for me. She tells Robert that I am disgustingly fat, and that from now on there will be no breakfast and no dinner, just a mid-afternoon sandwich and glass of milk.

Mr. Wesson is almost never home. He is often gone on business trips that last days. Now and then, he takes Robert, Anthony, and me on his day trips to sell Xerox machines. I like these days because he always stops twice to eat. I wish he would take us more often.

It is now August 1970, and the silence continues. I have tried everything to please Mrs. Wesson. I stay away from the townhouse from the time I get up until seven or eight at night, except for my brief visit to eat my sandwich and drink my glass of milk. I am so hungry and thirsty. It is hot here in Kansas, and my long pants and long-sleeved shirt don't help. They are getting bigger and baggier every day, so it's clear I am losing weight.

There is something called "the club" that's part of the townhouse complex. There's a pool outside it, and Mrs. Wesson goes there every day. She sunbathes and reads a book while the babies play in the sandbox and Robert and Anthony swim. I watch them from the club window, but I never go near them, because I don't want to embarrass Mrs. Wesson. A nice old couple works at the club, keeping it clean. They see me hanging around and ask me who I am. I say that I'm a foster kid with nothing to do, and that I'm really thirsty. They give me a quarter for the soda machine. We talk some more, and they say if I wipe off the tables for them so they can set up this thing called Happy Hour, I can have all the soda and peanuts I want. Happy Hour is apparently a time when adults can come and drink alcohol for free. I ask them questions about alcohol, and they say that if people drink too much of it, they lose control of themselves. I decide I must never start drinking, because I already have so little control over my world.

From time to time I look down from the club's big window at the families sitting around the pool. They seem part of a different world from the one I live in. I feel I am a total disaster, the opposite of everything a mother could have hoped for in a daughter. I wonder if my own mother in heaven thinks I'm as backward as Mrs. Wesson thinks I am.

Days go by and I walk the streets of Wichita. Unlike St. Louis, this place seems to have no parks or mobile libraries. I have nowhere to go. I can't stay in the townhouse. The pool is off-limits, because I'm a freak and I would embarrass Mrs. Wesson. The nice older couple works at the club only on Thursdays and Fridays. So I just walk mile after mile, every day. As I walk I review my life, trying to understand how I have failed so disastrously. Nothing is going right for me, and I don't know what to do.

The heat of summer is finally easing. In three weeks school will begin. I hear Mrs. Wesson on the phone with her friend. She says she will be taking Robert and Anthony shopping for school clothes, but not me. "If the social workers want her to go to school, let them come out here and take care of her," she says. This scares me badly. School is the only place in my life where I know any success. If that is taken away from me, my failure will be complete.

Something bad is happening to the body again. Oozing sores have broken out up and down my legs. I count twelve on the right leg and ten on the left. They are about the size of a quarter, and they seep blood and yellow pus. I try not to touch them, but they itch unbearably. No one notices them under the long pants I wear every day. I don't dare tell Mrs. Wesson, because I can't bear any more condemnation about how weird and different I am. All I can imagine is that I have leprosy. I have read about lepers in the Bible, and about how only Jesus would touch them. Maybe Mrs. Wesson has always known that I am a leper, and that's why she won't touch me.

Eventually the sores scab over and begin to heal. They still itch terribly, but I will myself not to feel the itchiness. I have other things to worry about besides leprosy. I am so hungry. It has been four weeks since we moved into this townhouse and Mrs. Wesson stopped feeding me, except for the daily sandwich and cup of milk. What I am allowed to do is come home around three o'clock and look in the kitchen window to see if the food is sitting on the table. Then I go in and eat and leave again right away. I never touch anything in the kitchen, because that would be stealing.

I tell myself I should be satisfied with what I have, but my stomach aches with hunger and makes noises like rocks rumbling together. There are two weeks to go before school starts. I can't take this anymore. I begin going to the local grocery store, pretending I'm looking for something to buy. Of course I have no money. As I walk up and down the aisles, I secretly open a cake or other perishable item and eat as much of it as I can. I vow someday that I'll pay the store back for what I am stealing. I know that I am breaking the law and a commandment, but I can't worry about that now. Someday I will be rich and no one will ever starve me again, but in the meantime, I need to eat.

The struggle for my soul is on. I am obsessed with thoughts of how to stop this emotional battering. I find myself staring at tall buildings, thinking how easy it would be to step off a tenth floor balcony and fly from this existence into the next. I am constantly thinking of the pros and cons of staying in this world or leaving it. The end seems to be beckoning me, luring me to give up.

It's so strange to think that I started this life as a beloved child, but after fourteen years, I am a pariah, an embarrassment to everyone. The only two people I can talk to are my mother, who is dead, and God, who won't use His great power to make people care about me. I'm on the edge of a cliff, just looking for a reason not to step into the oblivion of death.

It is a few days later. I have found the reason that I need. God and I have had a talk. I realize now that all my planning in the world can't make people care about me. I also know that even God can't change the hearts of people who are determined to do their own will. I've realized something else. God gets blamed for lots of stuff that people do, or fail to do. I wish I could tell my mother about all the bad things that adults tell me are God's will. "It's God's will that your mother died," they say, or "If God wanted you to be adopted, you would be." Bad things do happen in life, but it's at those times that other people should step in, if only because it's the right thing to do.

The result of my realizations is that, no matter how seductive I find the pull of a tall building, I will not go there again. I cannot destroy the gift of life that my mother gave me, nor the gift of free will that God gave me. If I die by my own hand, it will be because I allowed others to use their free will to destroy me. I cannot let them triumph. That would be letting evil win.

Something has to change soon. School has started for Robert and Anthony, but Mrs. Wesson has not sent me. It is incredibly lonely in the neighborhood for a fourteen-year-old, when the rest of the world is at school. I don't know what to do with myself. Once again I hear Mrs. Wesson on the phone, talking about "the foster kid" and how she doesn't want the responsibility for me. "Let the social worker come and get her," she says.

The neighbors have noticed that I'm not going to school. Today, as I sit on the steps of the townhouse, I hear one of them tell another that she has filed a report on me. She says she doesn't like the way Mrs. Wesson treats me, leaving me alone day after day. "She wears the same clothes every day, and you can see she's losing weight," she adds.

It is so unusual to hear anyone notice me or defend me. Why can't people like this neighbor be foster parents? She would probably hate me if she knew me, but she might like another kid.

Mrs. Wesson is mad tonight. For the first time in a long time, she speaks directly to me. She says that some nosy neighbor has reported her, and that the social worker is coming tomorrow. She says she'll be happy to see me go because I am a total failure.

I sit there and listen to her words, but I pull down the steel doors inside my mind so she can't hurt me.

All night, I stay awake wondering how to make a difference in this crazy world of foster homes. I wonder how many other kids in America live in this limbo and hate it as much as I do. I have heard about how people hijack planes so they can hold a news conference about something that is wrong. I fantasize about hijacking a plane myself. If I had all those cameras and reporters there, I would tell America about the consequences of abandoning its unwanted children to the shuffle madness that is foster care.

The social worker arrives. She and Mrs. Wesson sit down on the beautiful chairs in the living room. I have never been allowed in the living room. As I stand outside the room and listen, the social worker says she has received several reports about me being out all hours of the day, and sitting for hours on the steps alone at night.

Mrs. Wesson answers that she doesn't want me, and demands that the social worker return me to Scranton. The social worker says she needs a day or two to make travel arrangements. Mrs. Wesson says she wants me to leave the house tomorrow, while her sons are at school. She reminds the social worker to keep her in mind if a baby girl becomes available.

I just stare at the floor, my arms folded across my chest, trying to become invisible. The social worker warns me not to run away before tomorrow, when I will be returned to the orphanage. I mumble that I won't. Where would I run? As she leaves, she says she would like Mrs. Wesson and me to express ourselves clearly tomorrow, so that there can be "closure." I don't know what she means by that, but Mrs. Wesson says she will have plenty to say.

Tonight I can hear the Wessons having a heated discussion upstairs. When it is over, the light flips on in the basement and Mr. Wesson comes downstairs. He sits at the edge of the sofa bed, where James and John are already asleep. He says he understands I am going back to the orphanage. "I know things haven't been easy for you here, and I'm sorry," he says. "You have to understand that my wife has been under a lot of pressure. When you're married and have children, you'll understand that things like this happen." He adds that I shouldn't take this personally—that his wife really had her heart set on a baby girl. He says he's sure there is another woman somewhere who will want to be my mother. With that he wishes me luck, shuts off the light, and goes upstairs.

Is this what adults mean by "closure"? Am I supposed to feel better? What does he mean, I shouldn't take it personally? How else should I take it?

I dread tomorrow. When it comes, my dream of being part of a real family will die forever.

When I get up, Mrs. Wesson tells me to put on the same shirt and pants I was wearing when I arrived in her home nine months before. She saved the outfit just in case I didn't work out. I may not leave with anything she bought for me, not even the clothes on my back.

I have been wearing the same clothes for eight weeks, even to bed. There is a washing machine here, but I don't know how to use it. Sometimes at night, I wash my underwear by hand so I won't smell bad. My old clothes from the Smiths are baggy, because I have lost so much weight. They are too short as well, so I guess I've grown taller. I will leave this foster home with nothing but the clothes I arrived in.

I sit on the outside steps, waiting. I am so hungry, but Mrs. Wesson won't give me breakfast. Finally the social worker pulls up. She asks why I'm sitting on the steps wearing clothes that don't fit me. I explain about the clothes, and tell her I'm never allowed in the house. She tells me to come inside with her to talk with Mrs. Wesson. I don't want to go. I have a very bad feeling about this.

Mrs. Wesson and the social worker sit on the pretty chairs again, while I stand near the top of the basement steps. The social worker explains that she has my airplane ticket in her hand, but that before I leave, she thinks it's important that Mrs. Wesson and I tell each other what's on our minds, "so there won't be any hard feelings."

Mrs. Wesson launches into a tirade. She begins by reminding us that she never wanted me, but did me a favor by trying me out. "But she's not a girl; she's some sort of a freak," she spits out. "She's like a robot with no emotions. She's dead, but still breathing. It's a good thing her mother is dead," she says, "because she could never be a real daughter to anyone."

At this point the social worker interrupts, saying that Mrs. Wesson mustn't speak to me like that. "You told me I could say what I wanted!" Mrs. Wesson snaps, and the social worker lets her go on. I drift out of my physical body and hover in the air, watching myself try to fend off the punches that are flying at me thick and fast.

"No one's ever going to want this girl," Mrs. Wesson rages on. "The sight of her disgusts me. She can barely hold a conversation; all she can do is read. If her own mother came back from the dead, she'd be repulsed by what she's become. Get her out of here!"

The social worker asks if I have anything to say. I fly back to the body and shake my head no. She tells me to wait by the car and that she'll be right there.

Ten minutes later she comes out, her face red. As we drive to the airport, she tells me not to take what Mrs. Wesson says personally. My soul has been shredded by what I've heard, but I'm not supposed to take it personally. The social worker begs me to tell her what I'm thinking. I tell her not to worry about anything; just to get me back to the orphanage. She sighs in frustration. "I'm so sorry that Mrs. Wesson said those awful things to you," she said. "If it's any comfort, I can promise you that she will never get a baby, or any other child, from our agency." I tell her again not to worry; that it's not important.

I say goodbye to the social worker and board the plane. Sitting scrunched up against the window, trying to become invisible, I feel kind of sorry for her. She seemed like a nice lady, and she probably thought this "closure" thing was a good idea. It might be OK for adults, but I don't think it works between adults and kids. Kids are pretty powerless, while adults can build up or tear down what little there may be left of a kid's self-image.

The plane is leaving the ground. I have a five-hour trip in which to plan the rest of my life. I have already decided that I will never return to a foster home. Another time, I might not be able to stop the slide over the edge of my emotional cliff. I will live at the orphanage, because I can survive there. The nuns won't nurture me, or love me, or become attached to me, but neither will they heap abuse on me. Maybe life is full of trade-offs like that.

I just hope that God knows that all this was never about Him giving me too much stuff to carry. It was always about other people who kept piling it on.

As usual, when faced with moments of crisis in my life, I make a list. At the age of fourteen, flying somewhere over the United States during the first week of September 1970, I make a list of how I plan to survive.

1. I will never be a woman. Since my mother died, no one has come along to help me learn the necessary progression: from female, to girl, to woman. I've lost

my chance. I was a girl once, but now I'm nothing.

2. I will never deal with the body. I will divide myself into parts. The spirit part is good, because God and I are buddies. The mind part is good too, because teachers like me and tell me I am smart. But the body just complicates things. I will not let it affect me or acknowledge its existence. I will be just a person of spirit and mind.

3. I will never marry or have children. Mrs. Wesson is right: no one could ever marry a thing like me. I am a nothing, a broken person. How could I ever be someone's wife? How could I be a mother?

4. I will never cry. It isn't that I don't feel tremendous sorrow. But I can't allow myself to be swallowed up by an ocean of tears. I would drown.

5. I will never feel. I was not prepared for what happened this morning at Mrs. Wesson's house, and I let it hurt me. From now on I resolve to wear an invisible shield, so when people say hurtful things, they will slide off me into a place where I can deal with them later.

6. I will never tell anyone about my life. I'll be starting high school when I return to the orphanage. I will just tell

people that my family is dead, and that there was no one who could take me. That's all they need to know. No one really wants to know what happened, how it felt to me, what I yearned for. Why would I want anyone to know what a freak I am?

7. I will never depend on anyone. When I think back to the summer with the Wessons, it is the lack of food and water and the humiliation of wearing one set of clothing that stings me the most. I will become completely independent of other people, both physically and emotionally.

8. It is time for me to let go of those people who let go of me long ago. Keeping them alive in my heart only interferes with my ability to move on from the past. I am hereby releasing:

- My biological father. He abused my mother and her children. He never became my daddy.
- Daddy, who left us emotionally and physically. Once my mother was no longer here, he wasn't strong enough to protect us. His failure to protect us is unforgivable. Allowing us to love him, if he didn't love us, was unforgivable.

- Daddy's family, particularly Grandma
  Resuba. Instead of becoming the
  blessing that grandparents are supposed to be, she tried her best to
  destroy us.
- The police in Scranton, Pennsylvania.
  They allowed Grandma Resuba to
  terrorize us, and they did nothing.
- My foster families. They never
  opened their homes to me; to them,
  I was always an unwelcome outsider.
- My mother's family. It was as if, when
  my mother died, we ceased to exist.
  So now they won't exist in my heart.
- Finally, my mother. It is no sin of
  hers that has placed her on this list;
  it is only my need to accept her
  death and let her go in peace. She
  must live in her world, and I must
  find a way to live in mine.

The pilot is on the intercom. He announces
that we are landing at Newark Airport and
reminds us to fasten our seatbelts. I fasten mine
and ask God to give me the courage to survive
these coming years.

The social worker picks me up, and we stop
at McDonald's for dinner. She comments that
I seem to have lost a lot of weight. Back on the
highway, she peppers me with dozens of

questions. What happened in Kansas? Why did Mrs. Wesson send me back in those clothes? She asks me to tell her what Mrs. Wesson did and said. I tell her I can't talk about it. She says that she is looking for a new foster home for me, but I tell her that I will never go to another foster home; that I want to stay at the orphanage until I graduate from high school. She promises that she can find me a good home; one that doesn't want a baby or a different kind of child. I tell her no; I would not survive another foster home.

What she doesn't understand—what none of these social workers seem to understand—is what it's like to be stuck in this revolving door of foster care. I have no interest in going back on this assembly line in hopes that I will stick somewhere until I am eighteen. This is a poor substitute for actually looking for an adoptive home for someone like me. It is better to live at the orphanage. There I will have no hopes or expectations; I will know the score. I tell her that all I want to do is be left alone and go to school. I will not cause anyone any problems. I beg her not to look for another foster home for me. She says she'll think about it.

$\mathcal{B}$ACK AT THE ORPHANAGE

AGES 14 *to* 17

$\mathcal{D}$ear Mother,

As we travel up the long, winding driveway to the orphanage, I realize that this fortress-like building is to be my home for the next four years. In the darkness it seems grim and forbidding, but if I am to survive, this is where I must live.

There is a new charge person who meets us at the door. She offers to shake my hand, but I tell her I don't like to be touched. I think it is best to be upfront about that, because I know it is wrong to touch someone like me, even with a handshake. She pulls her hand back, then catches me up a bit on what's new at the orphanage. There are almost two hundred children here, but I am the oldest girl. The same elderly nun is in charge of the girls but she isn't well, so my help will be appreciated. Tomorrow I will catch the bus at the bottom of the hill and start classes at North Pocono High School.

The old nun who supervises the girls is called to the office. When she sees me she says, "The widow child is back!" and hugs me. I cringe from her touch, but I remind *myself that she is an old woman who means no harm.*

Well, God and Mother, how do you think I am going to survive here? Will anonymity be enough to save me?

Love,

Jerri

The old nun is happy to see me, because I have always been helpful and cause no trouble. She has been away for a long time, recovering from a heart attack. I decide that, since I am the oldest girl, I will try to help her out. She shows me where I will sleep in the dorm, then takes me to the storage room. Inside there are piles of donated clothes, along with supplies of soap, shampoo, and other items. She shows me a stack of pads "for your period" and tells me to take whatever I need.

I ask the nun how I can help her, and she tells me to wake the girls up every morning. She controls the lights in the dorm from her bedroom. We agree that she will flip the lights twice from her room. I am a light sleeper, so that will easily waken me. I will then get all the girls up; kneel and say morning prayers with them, and tell them to get dressed. I'll then go to the dining room to set up breakfast.

This is all fine with me. It helps fulfill my goal of being good and helpful. And at least I will have free access to the supplies I need, and I don't have to talk to anyone about them. Maybe "my period" means the blood. I will stockpile pads in case I am moved before I go away to college.

Lying in bed my first night back at the orphanage, I am surrounded by people, but I feel so alone. It has been a long day since leaving Mrs. Wesson's house this morning. As I lie here, I think of all the thousands of ways a person could fail. I try to focus on new goals, goals that will allow me to numb myself against any such failures. One such goal is to convince people that I am not intelligent after all. That's the only positive thing people ever say about me, and it might lead to my being acceptable to a foster home. In order to keep that from happening, I will try to learn all that I can in school while still keeping my grades low. I think I will purposely flunk every other test so that I will end up with a D average. Surely then I'll be safe from any foster home willing to "try me out."

Another of my goals concerns the library here at the orphanage. I love it. It is next to the beautiful chapel, and it must have at least a million books that tell a million stories about a million people. My goal, since I will be here for the next 1,460 days, is to read almost every single book in the library. I will start with the book on the bottom shelf on the right-hand side and keep going. When I read, I am transported through time and space to other worlds, worlds that offer me a glimpse of the lives of people I have never known. I can leave the loneliness of this world and enjoy the adventure of being somewhere else. I think I like reading about history best, because it helps me learn how other people made decisions, good ones and bad ones, and managed their lives. Reading softens the sharp edges of my reality. For a few fleeting moments, it lets me live the lives of people in faraway worlds. Reading is like a Novocain shot to my soul. It numbs all my pain.

It is 3:30 a.m. and I have awakened from a nightmare. I dreamed my mother was at a campfire with her back to me, talking about saving the country. I tried to get her attention as she kept walking towards the campfire. Suddenly she became engulfed in flames, and I woke up screaming.

Such terrifying dreams are bothering me more and more. I can barely keep myself together during my waking moments, and now this. I dream of my mother burning, or of being in an orphans' zoo watching people walk by without choosing me, or of hurling myself off a cliff. I lie awake hour after hour, surrounded by fifty girls, telling myself what a baby I'm being, yet too afraid to go back to sleep. I count the moments until the lights flip twice, and finally it is safe to get up.

When I go to the dining room to prepare for breakfast, I meet a kid named Ronald. He is funny and I like him. As we set up the food line, he tells me that his mother was murdered. I am stunned with anger. At least my mother's death was an accident. How could anyone deliberately orphan children by killing their mother? I could find no forgiveness inside myself for any one who would commit such an act.

There is plenty of food for breakfast, and it tastes so good. The nun who is cooking makes sure that everyone has plenty. Last night, I picked out some clothes from the donation pile in the storeroom. I threw the outfit Mrs. Wesson made me wear into the trash. As I walk to the bus stop, I feel excited at the new beginning that is about to take place.

The bus delivers me to a long, L-shaped building that sparkles in the sunlight. In front is a huge parking lot, filled with fancy cars driven by the older kids. When I walk inside, I am awed by how new and clean everything is. In the office, I hand over a piece of paper with my name and address written on it, so I don't have to say out loud that I'm from the orphanage. A nice secretary gets me my class schedule. I'm in the college prep program, which pleases me, even though I must fail for now.

The halls are incredibly crowded. I shrink into myself and manage not to be bumped around too badly. A few kids snicker at my hand-me-down clothing, but I ignore them. In homeroom, I sit behind a really good-looking kid named Peter. He is tall, with blond hair and blue eyes. When he whispers to me, he has a deep voice, like a man's. He asks where I've come from, since school has already been in session for two weeks. I tell him I live at the orphanage because my parents are dead. He says he can't imagine losing his parents, because they are really nice and do everything for him. He doesn't make fun of my clothes, and he even helps me with my algebra. I've made a temporary friend. Maybe I can make more of them.

On the way home, I think how exciting and scary school is. Maybe I need to focus on people who are kind to me, like Peter and my English teacher. She is very pretty and tells me not to worry, that she'll help me catch up with the rest of the class.

After being at the orphanage for a few weeks, I've gotten into a routine. From the time I get up in the morning, I get breakfast ready, go to school, come home, serve dinner, do homework, and go to bed. I am busier than I've ever been, and I embrace the busyness with an almost frenzied fury. By staying active, I can sometimes keep the dark thoughts from overwhelming me. I struggle to stay focused on the here and now.

It is nighttime again, the loneliest time in the orphanage. I can hear the younger kids crying into their pillows. They cry over the people who couldn't, or wouldn't, pull themselves together enough to be there for their children. During those moments it's hard not to think about who I am, and how I've gotten here. It's so sad that no one but me hears them crying, least of all the people who placed them here.

At school, I continue making temporary friends that talk to me about class stuff. I like making these friends, because it proves to me that I am not a total human failure. These people like parts of me, even though there will always be limits to what they know about me. Peter talks to me every day. He likes to tell me about what his family did over the weekend.

The only things I don't like about school are gym and the bus ride. A boy who gets on the bus at my stop makes fun of me as we wait there together. He laughs at me for being an orphan and for wearing donated clothes. One of the nuns tells me he will improve as he grows up, and that he's only a freshman in high school. I don't say anything, but I'm also only a freshman and I don't make fun of anybody. I hate gym because I have to put on this stupid short uniform. But on the bright side, there is no swimming pool, and the teacher is very nice. Because of her, I climbed a rope halfway to the gym ceiling. This is a big accomplishment for a non-athlete like me.

Today at school, I overhear two girls making fun of another girl's looks. They say she needs to learn to use makeup. It makes me wonder if I am really as ugly as Mrs. Wesson and Grandma Resuba said I was. The nuns are always saying that looks don't count, but I hear so many messages that contradict that.

I never really look at myself, except to see if my hair looks halfway decent. Tonight after everybody goes to bed I stand in front of the mirror to see if I'm as ugly as I feel. Staring into the dimly-lit glass, I guess I can see what makes me look like an alien. My eyebrows are bushy, and my nose is still a little bit flat. There is the ugly scar on my lip that repulsed Mrs. Wesson. My cheeks are sunken in, and there is something slightly crooked about my mouth. Only my eyes seem to have some life in them. Maybe the nuns are right and looks don't mean anything. But I can't help thinking that if I were a real girl who looked more normal, maybe an adoptive family would have wanted me. I remember Billy saying that he remembered how beautiful our mother was. And yet she produced a daughter that looked like me.

I decide I will never again look at myself in a mirror, except to see if my hair is combed properly.

We were told today what grades would appear on our report cards. In most of my classes,

I got a D or C. My plan is working well. But there is a problem with English. In that class, I am getting an F. I talk to my teacher after class and tell her I have a score of 69.5, so I should earn a D. She says no, I have a 69.4, and she will not give me the tenth of a point. She tells me that because of my class participation, she knows I know the material. She asks why I pass half the tests, and fail the others.

I shuffle my feet and admit my plan: that I don't want to appear too smart, so that the social worker will leave me alone and not place me in another foster home. She asks me if I want to go to college. I say yes, it is what I dream about. She tells me that when colleges look at my high school grades, they will not want to see any F's. I promise her that I will pass all the tests from now on.

Then she tells me something that really surprises me. In the standardized reading test that all the freshmen took last month, I scored first or second in the comprehension part. All the teachers are talking about the gap between my high score and my low grades.

The teacher is angry that I have been deliberately failing tests. She says I am reading at the college level, and that I should not squander this gift. She adds that I should expect a lecture when I get home, because she has called the orphanage.

Sure enough, at the orphanage, I am ordered to the office. The charge person, the one who doesn't like me anyway, is sitting at her big mahogany desk. The priest, Monsignor, is there too. They lecture me together, reminding me that everything I do reflects back on the nuns and the orphanage. Seeing that my plan has failed, I promise them I will get nothing less than a B from now on.

By the time my freshman year of high school ends, I have managed to pull up all my grades.

About this time of year, we orphanage kids all become nosy. Most of the nuns are transferred to new positions in June, and a new set arrives for the summer months. Then in August, yet another group comes, and they stay for the next school year.

Although we are constantly told not to, we do become attached to some of the nuns. I wonder if that's why they are moved so often. It's especially hard on the little kids to see these women constantly disappear, after so many other people in their lives have vanished too. No one seems to realize this. We aren't regarded as regular kids, with regular feelings of affection and need. We're orphans, and the social workers tell us that we should only become attached to our flesh-and-blood families, as though we can switch our affections on and off like electric lights.

Sometimes I have to laugh at the things we are told. The charge person likes to say that the nuns have given up their whole lives for Jesus. The reason they don't have children, she explains, is so they can go on a moment's notice anywhere in the world to care for lost children. Then she goes on to tell us how lucky we are to have the nuns and Jesus to love us. She doesn't explain why the next group of lost children needs the nuns more than we do.

I don't expect the nuns to be like mothers to us. Life at the orphanage is always so hectic, with so many children, that nobody can get any individual attention. Everything we do, we do in groups. But the nuns are mostly very nice people, and we care for them. To have them constantly appearing and disappearing forces us to toughen our hearts just a little more.

Summer has begun, and I have more time to work on my reading list. So far I have finished three shelves of books in the orphanage library. This summer I will try to read my way through six more. The charge person tells me that there is a program that will pay me minimum wage for cleaning at the orphanage. I do a lot of that any-way, so I might as well get paid for it. We agree that she will set up a bank account for me, so that when I leave someday, I'll have a little money of my own. From then on, I am responsible for the dining room, two guest rooms, the priests' dining room, and a ten-foot-wide hallway that runs the length of the orphanage. As I clean, I have lots of time to think about my future. I become very focused on going to college and making something of myself. I have come to realize that I am completely in charge of my future. In a way, this is a freeing thought. There are no safety nets for me, but neither are there any limits or expectations imposed by others. I will be what I make of myself.

I turned fifteen last week. There is no celebration, no cake, no gifts, no cards, but I have learned to accept this as part of my reality. On the first Sunday of each month, all our birthdays are celebrated together, but it's not like what I hear the kids in school saying about their family parties. It's now been seven years since I saw my mother. I don't dwell on it too much, but still questions about "what if" or "what might have been" come into my mind. I find myself wondering what she would look like, or how her voice would sound.

My sophomore year begins today. I can't believe what happens. As the day begins, the principal's voice comes over the loudspeaker. He asks us to stand for a moment of silence. We are remembering a student who drowned over the summer. The student was Peter. I feel like I've been punched in the stomach. I feel so awful for his parents; they must be in such incredible pain. At least, they should have no regrets about things left unsaid, because Peter constantly talked about how much fun he had with them. Tonight, as darkness falls around me, I ache for this temporary friend who showed me kindness. I don't know if there is loneliness in heaven, but if so, maybe while my mother waits for her children and Peter waits for his parents, they could hang out together.

I have decided that this will be a better school year than last year. I have two really neat teachers who are opening up new worlds for me. First is my American History teacher. He is like a storyteller, pacing back and forth and recounting events in history as though they were part of a family tree, all interconnected. I guess that's why I love history: it's a soap opera of good guys and bad guys and all the guys in between. Every person's action has a reaction, and no one, good or bad, comes to power without a whole fascinating series of events leading up to that moment.

The other class I really like is my English class. This teacher has introduced me to the work of Flannery O'Connor, a Southern writer whose stories are about the need for each of us to be ready to grasp our "moment of grace." I like something that Mr. Wiseman said: that if we listen to the literature of the ages, we can hear the echo of all humanity.

It is 3 a.m., and the doorbell at the orphanage is ringing loudly. I hate hearing this, because I know it can mean only one thing: that an abandoned child is being dropped off. I go to the top of the steps and hear two children crying, asking for their mother. A police officer is with them. He explains to the charge person that a neighbor brought them to the station, saying that their mother had left them a week ago and never returned.

The little girl looks so scared as she grips her brother's hand. There are a thousand separations that begin when kids become wards of the state, and the first one occurs now, when the charge person sends the boy in one direction and the girl in another.

Sometimes I really hate people.

The charge person notices me at the top of the stairs and tells me to take the little girl and wake up the nun in charge of her area. I take her hand. She tells me she is five years old, and that her mommy went out with her boyfriend but didn't come back. I don't wake the nun, who is old and tired. I just slip a note under her door. Then I borrow a small pair of pajamas from the supply room and put the little girl to bed. She asks if her mommy is coming back soon. I tell her yes, as soon as she takes care of her business. She starts to cry again, and I tell her everything will work out, that her mommy loves her, even though I know that is a lie. I find a stuffed animal to give to her, then I sit by her bed until she falls asleep.

I go back to bed, but I can't sleep. How could any woman call herself a mother and just walk away? How dare she not listen to the tears her child is weeping!

So many of the children here have been orphaned by neglect, rather than death. One girl that I know tells me sometimes about her mother, who is an alcoholic. She says that when her mom is sober, she is really cool. She brushes her hair and takes her shopping and talks with her about all kinds of stuff. But most of the time she is drinking, and then she becomes someone else. The girl's father left long ago. The girl cried as she talked to me, wondering why she isn't more important to her mother than the bottle. I told her what I could: that maybe someday her mother will pull herself together, but in the meantime to remember this is her mother's problem, and not her fault.

I see how drugs and alcohol destroy the goodness inside of people. I still don't have an answer about how people change who don't even have a substance-abuse problem. Every second and fourth Sunday, from two to four o'clock, it's visiting time at the orphanage. Dad shows up every few months. I never expect him anymore. He says he is very busy working on the house, taking care of Alice, and helping his parents. I have stopped having expectations of people. That way I am not disappointed.

As the months go on, the gap that exists between my two worlds—the orphanage and school—becomes wider and wider. When I board the bus in the morning, I feel as if I am stepping into a space ship traveling into another galaxy. My two worlds never touch one another. No one at the orphanage has a clue as to who my teachers are, what I study, what my desires and ambitions are, or what a tremendous effort it is just to enter the foreign world of school. No one at school has a clue as to where I go every day, the constant reminders of what I lack, or my alien world of heartbreak and loneliness. As much as I try to resist the temptation, I still find myself comparing myself to the kids at school and finding myself coming up short. As I see them plan their activities, get involved in clubs, and balance their worlds of family, friends, and school, I feel so inadequate. Then I remind myself, who has lived for so long in a world empty of all those normal things, that I can't expect to be like other kids.

Some students from Marywood College and the University of Scranton are at the orphanage today. They are supposed to act as big brothers and sisters to the kids here. When I ask the charge person if I can go to the playground with them, she says that at fifteen, I am too old. She tells me it is the younger kids, especially the boys, who need the extra attention. I look out of the dining-room window and see the kids running around while the students set up a picnic. I remember when I was ten or eleven, I played outside like that with the college students. It was a welcome break from the world we all lived in.

As I watch, I think about what big brothers and sisters represent in children's lives. I wonder about Billy, my real big brother. It has been years since I have seen him. He was such a wonderful brother, the way he tried to protect us even when he was only ten years old. Our mother would have been so proud of him. Even when he ran away or stole food, it was only because he was trying to help us. I will always love and admire him for his strength and courage.

It is turning to winter again, and the winds are blowing hard outside one night when I hear a little girl, Joyce, crying in bed. I go to her and ask what is wrong. She says the family she has been visiting for weekends over the past few months wants to adopt her. To me, this is great news. Every time a child is adopted, it's sweet revenge against the people who have walked away from me. I ask Joyce why she is sad. She says the social worker won't allow the adoption, because she is black and the family is white. The social worker wants to place her in a black foster home.

This makes me so angry I want to scream. This little girl has found a family who loves her, and she loves them. She calls these people "mommy" and "daddy." What sense does it make to deny her a permanent home because of skin color? I tell her I don't understand adults, but that I will pray she can be adopted by this family. The choices being made for her, by people who don't love her or understand her, will shape the rest of her life.

When I think about it, even the term "foster home" makes no sense. To "foster" means to care for someone or something temporarily, for a short time. "Home" means more than I can express, because it goes far beyond the physical care of a child. A home is a place where a kid should feel safe and not wonder every day, "Is this the last day?" Home is where a kid works on life plans and dreams, which slowly become real, with parents along for the ride.

"Foster parents" is another contradiction in terms. Parents provide stability, permanency, and roots. None of those are compatible with foster. Maybe social workers should call these temporary placements "foster places" with "foster people." Those are more realistic terms, and they might motivate people to try to find permanent homes for kids caught in this shuffle madness. Don't they realize that the longer kids stay in foster care and orphanages, the harder it is for them to ever reconnect to ordinary life?

These are the kinds of thoughts that come to me as I'm trying to pass as a normal kid at school. As hard as I work to stay in the here and now, I still find myself spacing out and end up miles and years away, in the coal cellar or listening to Mrs. Wesson saying words that burn in my ears. In school, sometimes my temporary friends will snap their fingers in my face, saying, "Earth to Jerri!" and that will bring me back. I have to find better ways to handle these intrusions from the past, because they are happening more and more.

It is the holidays again, and most of the kids have gone home or are visiting host families. The charge person says she won't force me to visit anyone. I am hard to place because of my age, anyway. I stay at the orphanage with two nuns, who have to be here in case some children are dropped off. This time alone provides me with a chance to read and watch TV, because the elderly nun in charge of the girls has gone away. Her only fault, in my opinion, is that she only lets us watch TV on Sunday evenings. Then we watch *Bonanza* and *The FBI*. I discover another show called *The Waltons*. It's about a family of kids whose parents are their safety net, and everyone gets along.

At one of the little parties which people occasionally give for the orphans, I get a small transistor radio. I'm supposed to hand it in, but I hide it from the nuns. The kids in school have radios, and it is so small no one will notice it. I hope my mother and God don't think I'm a bad person. When I have a chance, I listen to country music. Those songs somehow remind me of the life I had with my mother. It's hard for me to remember much about her any more, but I believe she'd lived in a place called Hayden, Kentucky. I pay special attention when Loretta Lynn sings, because she is from Kentucky too. This country music soothes me with its stories of heartache, loss, pain, and joy. Someday I am going to Nashville to listen to this music sung live. I might even try to find the place called Hayden, Kentucky, just so I can breathe the same air that my mother breathed.

The other thing I really enjoy listening to on the radio are the Philadelphia Phillies baseball games. I like baseball because it reminds me of how I approach life. There can be two outs in the ninth inning, and two strikes, yet it's always possible for there to be a hit and a comeback win. That's how I see life. No matter how down I get, I can will myself to believe that tomorrow will be a different and better day. Even with all the outs and strikes against me, I can still get a home run, or at least a hit, in this game of life.

It is especially quiet at the orphanage tonight. Earlier today a girl ran away. She is twelve years old, and her mother is dying in a hospital in Scranton. She had been crying and begging to go see her mother, but the social worker hadn't been able to arrange it. When I talked to her she was almost hysterical with grief, saying she couldn't live without her mother and had to see her before she died.

I pray for this kid, whose family has allowed her to be trapped like an animal in an anonymous place like this during the worst time of her life. I hope that they won't find her until after she had reached the mother she is so desperately looking for.

My second year of high school is coming to an end, and in two months I will be sixteen. Time is marching on, but inside I often feel frozen at age eight. Recently I heard one of the nuns calling us "throwaway kids." She meant children like me, the ones no one ever comes back for. Just as used shoes can never be restored to look as if they haven't been worn, the broken hearts of the kids that live here can never be made entirely whole again. Nothing can ever restore the lost innocence, the love and trust, that all children are entitled to.

I know that within two years, I will be going away to college and leaving Scranton, Pennsylvania. I have decided that I will never return here. It is in my best interest to put this place behind me. I will act as though all that has happened since my mother's death was a nightmare.

Every Sunday morning, the charge person calls some of us down to the conference room so she can lecture us about how good we have it compared to people in real life. She calls this "group dynamics," and it lasts from 9 a.m. until noon. I don't know whose benefit these meetings are for, but I sure know I don't feel any better by the time she is finished. Today she is telling us how married people struggle hard to feed themselves and their children, while we lucky orphans get everything handed to us.

I look around this room at all the brokenness that meets my eyes. There is Ronald, whose mother was murdered, and me, who was orphaned not only through death but by abandonment. There is Sally, who is slightly retarded, and Joyce, who is the wrong color for adoption. Billy, who rocks a lot, sucks his thumb waiting for his mother to get out of prison. Maggie, who is ten, cries every night for her mother to come home.

I try not to let what the charge person says filter into my mind, but she really does annoy me when she preaches about how lucky we are to have plenty of food and water. She doesn't have a clue about the kinds of hunger a child can feel.

The last time she was lecturing us, I decided to do an adoption between the orphans. I wrote the document with the assistance of some of the children living here. I figure this is as close as I'll ever get to adoption. While she is going strong about how we have everything we need and shouldn't feel sorry for ourselves, I pass around the paper for the other kids to sign. It says:

From this day forth, I, _____, do adopt _____ as my brother or sister, bound by circumstances beyond the ordinary. Dates August, 1972. Witnessed by _____ and _____ and God.

We all know this is not a binding agreement, and that most of us will never see each other again after we leave this place, but for now, it is a nice diversion from our real life.

Back at school, most of my classmates are caught up in driving lessons, phone calls, and school activities. I know most people would think it's funny, but I have never used the phone, never spent a night at a friend's house, never gone shopping for clothes, and never joined an after-school club. I do belong to the library club, since it meets during school hours. Now the teacher is trying to get me to join the debate team, since I like to do research so much. I ask the charge person about the debate club, which goes to other schools and sometimes meets on Saturdays. She says it is OK as long as I can find my own ride. The debate teacher says she will take me to the mock trials. I feel strange having to depend on a teacher for transportation, but I work with what I have.

At school, I listen to stuff the kids talk about. There's a lot of it I don't understand, like talk of romance, or drugs, or weekend parties, but that's OK. I just stay quiet and try to guess at what I don't understand. But today in biology class, one of the girls makes fun of me. The teacher was explaining something about a frog, and when I ask how a frog knows when to give birth, the teacher says, "They're just like humans." I ask, "What does that mean?" The girl snickered and asked loudly, "Didn't your mother teach you anything about sex?" Everyone laughed at my expense. For the rest of the class, I couldn't hear anything the teacher said. I resolve never to ask another question in biology class.

Trevor's foster homes haven't worked out, and he's back at the orphanage. Lately the social worker has been pressuring Dad to take us to the house he has built twenty feet away from his parents'. He built it with the money the military pays for his dependents—us. Dad says he'll take Trevor temporarily, as Trevor is too old to stay at the orphanage. I definitely don't want to go.

Living with Dad beside the Resubas would be no better than a foster home—worse, because these people have already abused and neglected me, and never acknowledged that they've done anything wrong. Trevor doesn't want to go to Dad's house either, and I beg the charge person to let him stay, but she says no. Trevor tells me not to worry. He says that if Dad won't keep him or Grandma Resuba starts her nonsense, he will go on welfare, finish high school, and then join the Navy. He hugs me and wishes me good luck, saying he'll try to stay in touch.

As I watch Trevor drive away with the social worker, I know that the brother I've seen the most is leaving my life forever. We may meet again, but we have been ripped apart too many times. I hope he can hold on until high school graduation, and then follow his dream to a better life.

A few months later, Daddy comes for one of his rare visits. He says he's sorry things didn't work out at the second foster home. I tell him I'm fine staying at the orphanage, and that I plan to stay here throughout high school. Then he asks if I want to come to the house next week to visit Trevor. At first I don't know what to say. I don't want to see Grandma Resuba, but I love my brother. For two hours, how bad can it be?

Dad picks me up today for the visit. As we drive up, Grandma Resuba is standing on the porch. She asks me how I'm doing, as if I'd been away on vacation. I want to scream. Instead, I just give her a cold look and say, "OK." Grandma Resuba begins bragging to me how well Alice is doing. I think to myself, why shouldn't she be doing well? I don't blame Alice for anything, but I can't help but think how her well-being came at the expense of her brothers and sister. I can't listen to any more talk of how good she is compared to us. Grandma Resuba says Trevor has a "wild streak" in him, and that he must take after my mother. I just glare at her and tell her I am going to go see my brother now.

Trevor and I wander around the yard, and near the coal bank we meet an old neighbor, a boy my age. He was always nice and friendly, and was the only neighbor kid who hung around with us when we were little. He wants to show us some trails up near the mine shaft. Trevor has to do something back at the house, so I go with him alone. When we get to the back trails, he asks me if I want to "fool around." I look so startled that he realizes I don't know what he is talking about, so he goes on. "You know—we could kiss and fool around some like married people." I tell him no, let's go back to the house. He seems worried and apologizes for offending me. I tell him not to worry about it, but that I have a lot of stuff on my mind.

I don't tell him how confused I am about

what he is asking, since I don't know what married people do or what it has to do with kissing. I don't want him or anyone else to know what a freak I am.

When I get back to the house, Dad says he needs to get me back to the orphanage. I hug Trevor goodbye, as Grandma Resuba watches from the porch. Dad says he'll visit me soon, which means a few months from now. I decide inwardly I will never visit the house again. There is no place for me there. The truth is that there never has been, at least not since my mother died.

My senior year is starting, and I must get serious about my college plans. If only my mother could see me now, I think she'd be proud. I'm still here, I'm alive, and I'm making something of my life. I speak with clarity and pronunciation that is crisp and clear. Most people don't even notice that I once had a cleft palate—my nose is no longer flat, and there is only a tiny scar on my lip.

And yet there are frequent reminders that I am not like other people. Today I drive into town with a nun to help her carry supplies. On the way home in the dark, we pass a building with a red light on it. I remark on how pretty it looks, and say that when I build my log cabin in the woods, I'll put red lights on it too. The nun gives me a startled look and says, "Didn't your mother ever teach you anything? Red lights are for 'ladies of the evening.'" I turn red and shut my mouth, knowing that I've made another mistake. I have no idea what red lights or "ladies of the evening" mean, but I guess they have something to do with subjects like the body and sex and fooling around that are off-limits for me.

As we drive back to the orphanage, I think for the thousandth time how much I have to learn aside from book-knowledge. I can take care of the book stuff pretty well myself. Ever since I was in ninth grade, every time I got my hands on a few dollars I used the money to order paperback books. So far, I have amassed a collection of 350 books. There was a problem with where to put them, since my only storage space is a locker that is twelve inches wide and five feet high. But since I am in charge of cleaning the dining room, I know about the huge walk-in closet there, it's big enough to hold dishes for two hundred kids. I figure that, since I have to clean there, I'm entitled to fix the closet any way I want. So I've gradually transferred all the dishes to the floor, while I've given my books the place of honor on the shelves. There's a light in the closet, and when the craziness in the orphanage gets to be too much for me, I go in there, turn on the light, and read. By now in my senior year, all the dishes are on the floor, and almost every inch of shelf space is filled with my books.

When Sister Linda happens to open the closet door and sees my personal library, she almost has a heart attack. I point out that it contains many literary classics, but she still isn't happy, insisting that dishes don't belong on the floor. I tell her that stories and ideas are more important than old dishes, but she doesn't agree.

Finally, though, we reach an agreement. The dishes go back on the shelves, but she finds some old book cases that fit under the bottom shelf. I personally like my design better, but sometimes I must compromise and give in to the architectural ideas of others, especially if they are in charge.

It's time to take this thing called the SAT, or Scholastic Aptitude Test. It is a measure of how well I am supposed to do in college. All the college-bound kids at school are taking it together on a Saturday at the University of Scranton. I've managed to get the application sent in, after repeatedly asking the charge person for a special kind of money called a "check." There are so many things I don't know, even about different ways to pay for stuff. She gives me the check, but tells me it will be deducted from the money I get for cleaning. I don't care, because the money will help me accomplish my goal, which is to leave Scranton, go to college, and become a real person. I ask her next how I can get to the

University of Scranton for the SATs. She says I have to find my own ride because the orphanage cars have to be available for important things.

But there is this kid, Jake, in my trigonometry class, who I overhear making plans to take the SATs. I ask if he can give me a ride, and he says, "Sure, no problem." When I start to tell him where I live, he says he already knows. He's a handsome boy with long blond hair, gold-rimmed glasses, ruddy cheeks, and a very likable personality.

The SAT is a headache-maker. Afterwards Jake and I meet our other classmates outside the test room. They decide to go out for lunch before heading home. I don't have any money, because I never do, and it never occurred to me that people go out to eat after doing something big. I tell Jake that I'll wait by the car. But he says, "Come on, I'll treat you. My father gave me money for us both." We all have a good time at the restaurant. It's the first time I have ever been out with a group of students, and it feels OK. Gestures of welcoming kindness sometimes come when I least expect them.

After the SAT, it is time to fill out the college applications. I apply to Villanova University, near Philadelphia, and Alvernia College, in Reading, Pennsylvania. As I work slowly through the applications, I wonder why there are so many questions about my family background and family income. The charge person said not to ask her for any help, so I must answer the questions as best I can. When I look at all the blank spaces I am leaving, I realize the application looks as if I was never born or belonged anywhere. I decide to write a letter to go along with the applications, explaining that I am a ward of the state and live in an orphanage. I hope that will be OK.

Back at school, things are going pretty well. My biggest problem is harassment by the guidance counselor, Mrs. Crusher. She gets a thrill out of calling me to her office and making me feel lower than I already do. She asks me incredibly stupid questions, such as, "What did you do that you have to live at the orphanage?" When I explained that my mother died in a gas explosion and that my adoptive father didn't want me, she laughed in a sneering way. She said, "There must be something really wrong with you, if no one on either side of your family would take you."

What really makes me bristle is when Mrs. Crusher tells me how lucky I am to have clothing and food. She points out that no one really has to take care of me. The final straw comes when I ask her for the college forms I need. She raises her eyebrows and says, "You need to face the fact that you're not college material. Kids like you shouldn't take loans and scholarship money away from children with families."

At this I blow up. "What do you mean, 'kids like me'? You have no right to talk about the kids at the orphanage. You know nothing about them. You can call me names, tell me I'm a freak and too stupid to go to college, but don't you *ever* talk about the kids at the orphanage."

Mrs. Crusher gets all flustered, telling me that I'm a "defiant brat" who doesn't appreciate what I have. She says she will call the charge person and have my "act of disrespect" put in my permanent record. At the orphanage, we're always hearing how anything bad we do will go in our permanent record and follow us for the rest of our lives. Apparently nothing good is ever written there.

A few days later, Mrs. Crusher calls me in again. She says she has talked to the charge person at the orphanage and they have agreed Mrs. Crusher will give me a personality test to see if I am emotionally disturbed. I say I won't take it, but Mrs. Crusher tells me to remember that I could be moved at a moment's notice, to a different institution or a foster home. She would gladly use her power to inflict more damage on me.

"Fine," I say, "I'll take your stupid test. Both you and the charge person are cruel hypocrites. You've already decided I'm a failure." As I take the test, I make her even madder by muttering, "hypocrites, hypocrites!" under my breath. When I'm done with the test, she snatches it away and tells me she will share it with the charge person. Naturally, it will go in my permanent record. She adds that just by glancing at it, she can tell that I am a little disturbed in my mind. I tell myself that I'm not the only one.

Unfortunately, Mrs. Crusher is the gatekeeper of the college information, so I have to keep going to her office and asking for various forms. She loves to say as she hands them over, "Have your parents fill this out. Oh, I forgot— you don't have parents, do you? Well, I guess you'll just have to do the best you can on your own."

I will not let her see me break, but it eats at me that an adult gets a thrill out of heaping further humiliation on me.

Today in the school library, I read that we are getting out of the war in Vietnam. Orphans are being flown out of South Vietnam so they can come to America to be adopted.

At first, I feel resentful at this news. Only as I sit back and reflect do I realize that an orphan is an orphan. The nationality may be different, but the losses are the same. Anyway, kids like me who are available for adoption will never be taken because of our age, sex, color, disability, or a thousand other reasons. The people adopting these babies from Vietnam wouldn't give us a second look. And if they are caring enough to embrace any orphan from any place, that is at least one less lonely child. So I think I will follow this Operation Baby Lift story and cheer for every kid who gets out of Vietnam.

As I learn more about these babies, I develop a special feeling of camaraderie with them. They are half-Vietnamese, half-American, and they are called "the dust of the earth." The Vietnamese have a special scorn for them. I can relate to that, because if people believe they can love only their own flesh and blood, as Daddy's family did, nothing can make them change.

I am so excited! Today I got acceptance letters from both Alvernia College and Villanova University. I am so happy I dance in the dining room and run down the hallway to tell everyone I see. Just think, I'm going to college! Me, a ward of the state and nobody's child, is good enough and smart enough and alive enough to enter the land of the living. The daughter of my dead mother is really going to be somebody someday.

Better yet, a second letter comes, saying I have been awarded a grant for tuition, room, and board at Alvernia. If I maintain a "C" average, the grant is good for four years. Now it is official. There is nothing to stop me from pursuing my dreams.

The buzz at school lately is about a special dance called the "senior prom." Apparently, kids who go to it spend a lot of money, get a date, and have family over to the house to take lots of pictures. The girls wear evening gowns and the guys tuxedos. Even though this experience is not for me, I think it must be exciting for my friends. I wonder how they know how to date, how to dress, how to dance, how to do all these unfamiliar things. Sometimes I wonder what it would be like to be Cinderella for a night.

Once again, I am called to the charge person's office. These meetings always make me nervous. They rarely leave me feeling better about myself. I can't imagine what she wants, since I will be leaving so soon. I will graduate in three weeks, and then leave for college in August.

In her office, the charge person tells me I need to make arrangements to live somewhere for the summer. I am too stunned to answer. She explains that the day after my high school graduation, the orphanage's contract for my care will expire. I tell her that I have nowhere to go, no one who wants me. I plead with her to allow me to stay, just until college starts. She says no, that once I have graduated from high school, I am no longer a ward of the state.

Still almost speechless, I manage to ask where I will go. She says that I'm an adult now and have to make my own plans. She does say that she's called Daddy's family, but that they aren't interested in having me. Also, she says, I have $1200 in the bank from the cleaning I have done. She finishes by saying it will be best for me to learn to be independent and find my way in the world.

I leave the office shaken. As I go upstairs, Sister Linda and Sister Kate ask what the charge person wanted. When I tell them, they are furious, and head back down to the office. I hang over the railing and listen to the argument that follows.

"You can't put that child out like this!" one of the nuns exclaims. "If we're not legally responsible, we're morally responsible for giving her a home. She has no place to go. She certainly can't go back to that idiot family of hers. How can you deny her just three months here, until she has a place to go?"

The charge person answered angrily. "How dare you speak to me like that! Jerri is seventeen, and it's time for her to live on her own." She orders them not to bring up the topic again.

I meet the nuns in the dining room. They are both beet red with rage. Sister Kate tells me not to worry. Her grandmother has an extra bedroom, and I can rent it for the summer. Both of them tell me just to focus on final exams and graduation, and they will make all the arrangements. I feel very lucky to have guardian angels like them, who occasionally step in and help me along the road of my life.

What does the charge person mean by saying I'm an adult now? The day after my graduation, will I know everything I need to know in order to run my life? Will my classmates, too, become instant adults at seventeen and no longer need their parents? Somehow I doubt that. But once again, the rules governing my life seem to be different than the rules that apply to normal people.

All the high school seniors and their parents are invited to a dinner dance at a local country club. A friend encourages me to go, saying her parents will drive me there and back. I ask the charge person if I can go. She says yes, and that I should pick out a dress from the donation pile in the storage room.

I am excited about going to my first and last school event. The only problem is the dress. The one I found is green and looks like it is made of old curtains. A friendly nun tells me it looks hideous, and to ask the charge person for money to buy a gown. As much as I hate asking her for things, I do ask, and sure enough she says no. She tells me to be thankful there are donated clothes to pick through. "Besides," she adds, "you don't want to look too fancy."

Once again, my guardian angels, Sister Kate and Sister Linda, come to my rescue. They go shopping and buy me a pretty pink dress. They tell me not to let the charge person know, and that I should enjoy myself at the dance.

When I arrive at the country club, it is more beautiful than I ever imagined. The tables are covered with crisp white tablecloths and decorated with bright flowers. Almost everyone in my class is here with his or her parents. I don't think I've ever seen so many parents gathered together in one place. I sit back and savor the moment, watching the enjoyment of my classmates. I have a good time, and I believe that someday I will be in a room of people who are connected, in some way, to me.

But later, lying in bed reflecting on the evening, I fight to keep tears from overwhelming me. Seeing so many parents lovingly interacting with their children almost broke me in half. Sitting with my friends, I felt like an intruder, spying on a normal world that to me is totally foreign. I am amazed to see the nurturing care that parents still lavish on their seventeen- and eighteen-year-old children, even though they will be adults soon. In less than a week I will graduate from high school and leave the only home I know, forever.

I will rent a room in Sister Kate's grandmother's house for twelve weeks. She is charging me twenty-five dollars a week.

I have a job lined up with CETA, a government program that helps people get a foothold in the job market.

These are good things. I try to tell myself that.

But I am terrified. I want my mother. I am not equipped to face this unknown world.

Tonight Sister Linda and some of the other nuns give me a surprise graduation party. The charge person didn't want me to have one, but she is gone for the weekend. Sister Renee has baked a cake, and there is soda for everybody. I get a dictionary as a gift from the whole group. I'm going to keep this dictionary forever. It represents contributions from so many of the kids, and even some of the nuns. Nobody really has any money.

The charge person found out about the party. She is angry and says she won't attend my graduation. The nuns tell her I hadn't known anything about the party and that she shouldn't blame me, so she changes her mind. I don't care, though, if anyone attends the ceremony at school, because my little party was great. Simply having a cake and some root beer and receiving a gift meant so much to me. It was public acknowledgment of a job well done. I like to think that if the other orphans see that a "throwaway child" like me can make it out of the system, there are opportunities for them to succeed as well.

As I approach graduation, I realize what a safety net school provided for me. For the most part, I was able to blend in and act like a normal person, even though I knew I wasn't one. Through my involvement in the library club, I became organized and resourceful. Books helped me realize how large the world was. Other students would actually ask me for help on a project or want to know how to find a certain book, and I knew the answer. The debate club helped me learn how to do research and find the answers to many questions. School has allowed me to succeed and to see concrete proof that I am not stupid. From my freshman English teacher who refused to let me settle for less than my best, to the gym teacher who taught me how to climb a rope halfway to the ceiling, to my upperclass English teachers who taught me about the literature of the ages, to my history teacher who recommended me for history contests, I owe many people my gratitude.

Report cards came today. I have come a long way since my freshman year, when I nearly failed everything on purpose. Now I've got five A's, two B's, and a C+ in math. Not bad for a nobody. Back at the orphanage, I show it to people. Sister Linda tells me I am smarter than I realize. The charge person says she hopes this good report card "isn't just a fluke." No matter. I show it to the other orphans and tell them the best way to get back at people who have done them wrong is to do well in school in spite of them. In two days, these fellow orphans will be gone from my life forever. I hope they will be tough enough not to be crushed by what life has to hand out to them.

Today I sat at the end of the row at graduation. It is not easy having the last name of Zigga, because I'm frequently last in line. The charge person came, along with Sister Linda, Dad, and Jennifer, a former nun who is a friend. The charge person said I had to invite Dad because he is my legal guardian. It's been nine months since I've seen him.

It is hard for me to concentrate on the ceremony. All I can think about is that in twenty-four hours, I will leave everything and everyone I have ever known. My inner conversations with my mother and God will be the only constants in my life.

I have been handed my diploma. Most of my classmates are going to big family celebrations, where they will receive congratulations and gifts. A few of them are even getting cars. Many are leaving for something called senior week.

Outside of the high school, Dad wishes me good luck and goes to his car. He waves as he drives away. I go back to the orphanage and show the kids my diploma. The little ones are impressed and tell me that they are going to get one someday, too.

Late that night when everyone is asleep, I go through the donation pile of clothes and pick up a few pants and shirts that might fit me. Then I pack them and my few belongings into two cardboard boxes. Most of the space in them is taken up by books I couldn't leave behind. The charge person has given me my savings passbook. It says that I have $1200 in my account. That sounds like a lot of money. I figure I'll be able to live on that for the next four years, until I'm out of college.

I ask the charge person if I can come back to visit occasionally. She says no; that it's best if I just make a clean break, forget about the past, and make a life for myself. She tells me that people won't be interested in what has happened to me, and that if I tell them they may think I'm a bit strange.

It's moving day. Although I am now a high school graduate and supposedly an adult, I don't feel any more grownup than I did yesterday. I just feel like a seventeen-year-old kid, unwanted and scared. Sister Kate and Sister Linda drive me to Sister Kate's grandmother's house. They visit with the old woman for a while, then wish me luck and say goodbye. They promise they'll keep in touch, and then they are gone. With them go the last people who know the world I've come from, or understand a little of what I've been through these last ten years. Now I am expected to know how to function in this ordinary world.

Lying alone in bed, feeling so confused and alone, I decide the way to survive this transition is to become an observer of life, rather than a participant. At present, I don't know enough about this world to take part in it. Maybe if I watch people long enough, I will learn to act and even feel like they do. As scared as I am, I realize that I have an opportunity to make a fresh start. I will try to look at the world as if I were seeing it for the first time. At the same time that I am becoming more book smart, I will try to become more people smart as well.

The summer weeks fly by. I work in a factory, doing the same task over and over. Dad works there too, but he hasn't told anyone that I'm his daughter, at least in the legal sense. I use the money I earn to pay my rent and eat out, because I don't know how to cook and I don't have anywhere to keep food. I've rented only a room, not a kitchen.

I spend a lot of time reading in my room. My favorite book is *Death Be Not Proud*. It's about the relationship between a teenage boy who is dying of a brain tumor and his family. I've read it eight or nine times, and each time I find something new in it. The kid fights so hard to live, and his parents do everything possible to nurture him and find help for him. He ends up dying, but what an extraordinary life he lived because of his ability to touch people. He really made a difference.

I want to make a difference, too: not by dying of a brain tumor, but by living in such a way that the world is a better place because of my existence. Right now sitting in the lonely city of Scranton surrounded by my boxes, it doesn't seem that I've accomplished much.

Tomorrow is the day that begins the rest of my life. I truly believe that I will flourish in college. Finally I will be with people who appreciate my mind, and who are not part of the system that has tried to label me a failure. As I prepare my few possessions for the trip from Scranton to the city of Reading and Alvernia College, I feel nothing but eagerness to leave this city that has been the site of so much pain. I know it's unreasonable to blame the city itself or the good people that probably live here, but all I have ever known here is grief and rejection. Trevor says he wants nothing to do with the state of Pennsylvania; he just wants to start a new life somewhere else. As soon as he finishes high school, he will join the Navy. It has been years since I've seen Billy or Tyler. It's too bad that our shared grief has splintered us, rather than drawing us closer together. It's as if we've needed to use all our little stores of energy to heal ourselves, rather than maintain bonds with one another.

I will enter Alvernia College as though I am

newborn into this world. No one needs to know anything about my past. I will just tell people that my parents are dead and that my family lives far away. No one needs to know what a freak I am.

As I wait at the Greyhound station, my one-way bus ticket in my hand, I can't stop looking at my fellow travelers' suitcases. I guess they do look better than the battered cardboard boxes I am clumsily lugging. The taxi ride to the station was expensive, almost seven dollars. I need to be careful with my money, or my $1200 won't last four years. I didn't manage to save anything from my summer factory job. It all went for food and rent and this bus ticket, plus I gave some to Trevor.

I settle into my window seat and the bus begins its journey. The countryside is so beautiful. It makes me think how nice it would be to really travel someday. This is only a two-hour trip, but I wish it would go on forever. Once I arrive in Reading, I'll have to summon up all my courage to face my fear and the unknown.

$\mathscr{T}$HE COLLEGE YEARS

AGES 17 *to* 24

$\mathscr{D}$*ear* Mother,

The taxi that will take me to Alvernia College is finally here. I put my boxes in the trunk, because the driver says he can't lift heavy loads. All those years of cleaning at the orphanage have gotten me used to lifting.

As we enter the grounds of the college, I marvel at its beauty and thank God I was able to stick to my goals. Here, no one will know I was never normal enough to have an ordinary family. Here, all that will count is my ability as a student. I have in mind exactly what I will tell people:

> I am from upstate Pennsylvania, but traveled a lot because my parents were in the military.

> My parents are dead and I have no living relatives, except for brothers whom I haven't seen for years.

I will never tell anyone about foster care, the orphanage, or the coal cellar. I'm afraid no one would accept me as a friend if they knew my history of rejection. I want people to like me, not be repelled by me.

Mother, if you were alive and knew the whole truth about me, would you continue to be proud of me?

Love,
Jerri

As I get out of the taxi and pay my bill, a student named Becky comes to greet me. She is from the college welcoming committee. I grab my boxes and follow her into the dorm, where I am introduced to the nun in charge of student life. Becky shows me to my room, which I'll share with another student. I put down my boxes and notice how little space they take up. I sure don't have enough things to fill the closet or drawers allotted to me.

Becky gets me started on a campus tour. Other students are arriving with their parents. Mostly what I notice is their pretty suitcases. None of them seem to be arriving alone, or by taxi, or carrying cardboard boxes. I can't do much about the parent part, but I tell myself next time I move somewhere, I will have a proper suitcase.

Next there is a picnic for incoming freshmen. It is so nice that I have trouble believing I belong here. People are introducing themselves by shaking hands. Apparently this is standard practice among ordinary human beings. Even though I don't like to be touched, I force myself to do the same. There is plenty of food and everyone is talking at once. For the first time, I feel like it is OK to talk about how excited I am about being here. I tell people I am going to study history and hope to become a lawyer or a missionary. I am asked a thousand times where

I've come from, so I go into my rehearsed story:
My parents were in the Air Force and died in an
accident. I'm not really from anywhere. I tell
them I don't like to talk about the past, but
want to focus on the future. I realize all this is
not entirely true, but it's close enough.

Back at the dorm, I arrange to have a private
room starting tomorrow. I tell the nun in charge
that I snore very loudly and don't want to dis-
turb a roommate. Again, this isn't entirely true,
but I don't want to create problems by telling
the whole truth. My roommate seems very nice.
It's just that she's got a *Playgirl* calendar tacked
to her wall with a picture of a naked man on it.
I never realized there was such a difference
between men and women. I don't say anything
of course, because at eighteen I should know so
much more than I do. Everyone who walks into
our room laughs and says that the calendar is
really cool. But it isn't just that that makes me
want to have my own room. It's that I don't
want anyone to find out about my awful dreams
and the fact that it can take hours for me to fall
asleep. At the orphanage, I often sat in the hallway by the night light, reading or thinking for
hours. In order not to draw attention to myself,
I'll need my own room where I can balance my
school life and my private world. I tell my roommate about the snoring and that I get up really
early to study. I don't mention the calendar,

because I don't want her to think I'm weird.

There is very little in this college life that resembles my experience as an orphan. On the outside, I am an eighteen-year-old adult, but the reality is that I haven't a clue about what I am doing or what I am supposed to be. It is like I am still eight, fast-forwarded through ten years without any ordinary developmental experiences. Eighteen going on eight is how I feel inside.

For instance, one of the neatest things about dorm life is that I have access to a TV any hour of the day or night. I have discovered that I love getting up Saturday morning and watching cartoons. I have never watched cartoons before, as far as I can remember. I am amazed by the creativity of people who can make a cartoon that is so bright, colorful, fast and funny. Sometimes I wonder if there is something wrong with me, liking to watch cartoons at my age, but I think I just want to experience what I have missed. Maybe by filling in some of those gaps, I can come close to catching up with kids that are my own age.

I am beginning to make some friends. One of them, Matthew, says he is going to be a psychologist someday. He loves to act and sing, and sometimes he'll play the piano over in the administration building and a bunch of us will gather to listen to him sing. One of my favorites is "The Wedding Song." It is about how adults learn to love one another with the blessing of God and other people. I think it must be really neat to have that kind of love.

I have met many orphans, but today Matthew introduces me to my first widow. Her name is Celeste, and she is returning to college to get her degree. When we meet, she reaches out to shake my hand. I say, "Please don't touch me," rather abruptly. She apologizes, but I explain that it's not her; I just have a thing about being touched. She has very kind eyes and a ready smile.

Celeste is studying history, like me, and I find out that we have a lot of classes together. Her children are still in middle and high school, so she has to work around them. Her husband died a few years ago and she is going to college in order to move on with her life.

Matthew and Celeste leave, and I sit on the grass thinking. When Celeste talks about her husband, I sense such pain and sadness in her. I guess that her son and daughter have helped her keep on going. I also sense that she loved on a level that I will never know, because she loved a man who was her partner and the father of her children. To have loved someone that intensely, and then for him to have died in the middle of their loving, must have shaken her world. I feel a kinship with Celeste. Maybe this is why Jesus madness. Don't they realize that the longer kids stay in foster care and orphanages, the harder it is for them to ever reconnect to ordinary life?

These are the kinds of thoughts that come to me as I'm trying to pass as a normal kid at school. As hard as I work to stay in the here and now, I still find myself spacing out and end up miles and years away, in the coal cellar or listening to Mrs. Wesson saying words that burn in my ears. In school, sometimes my temporary friends will snap their fingers in my face, saying, "Earth to Jerri!" and that will bring me back. I have to find better ways to handle these intrusions from the past, because they are happening more and more.

It is the holidays again, and most of the kids have gone home or are visiting host families. The charge person says she won't force me to visit anyone. I am hard to place because of my age, anyway. I stay at the orphanage with two nuns, who have to be here in case some children are dropped off. This time alone provides me with a chance to read and watch TV, because the elderly nun in charge of the girls has gone away. Her only fault, in my opinion, is that she only lets us watch TV on Sunday evenings. Then we watch *Bonanza* and *The FBI*. I discover another show called *The Waltons*. It's about a family of kids whose parents are their safety net, and everyone gets along.

At the Berkshire Mall I find a store called The Gap. I have never been clothes shopping before and I have no idea how it's done. I ask a sales lady to point out the women's section, and there I see some corduroy pants that look all right. The sales lady asks what size I wear. I have no idea. She tells me she thinks I'm about a size ten and gives me a pair to try on. I realize I am supposed to go into a dressing room. I turn red even at the thought of changing clothes there in the store, even though I realize no one can see me. I have tried so hard to pretend this body doesn't exist. I try on the pants, and they seem to fit. I tell the sales lady I want to buy one in each color. She says they come in fourteen colors, and I say that's OK, I'll take one of each. In addition, I try a shirt on and tell her to take one of each of them to match the fourteen pants. The lady keeps asking me if I'm sure, but I say yes.

The bill is almost $300, a lot of money out of my fund, but the clothes will last for four years. I'm left with only $900. It costs a lot to live in the real world.

I am slowly learning. A teacher has spoken to me, mentioning how I walk around staring at the ground and don't look at people when I talk to them. She tells me that she and the other instructors know where I've come from and they understand, but that other people will think I'm strange if I don't act more socially normal.

This is something I can practice. In my room I work on holding my head up and looking forward. It is difficult for me to look into people's faces, because when I do that I feel as though a giant spotlight is shining on me, showing everyone what a freak I am. But I will try hard, because it is important for me to blend in with these people. Their acceptance of me makes me feel better about myself.

I look at these people whom I am beginning to regard as friends. They seem to welcome me into their presence, even with all my limitations. I don't like to be touched; I don't want to talk about the past; I even have a lisp when I speak. And yet there are these people in my life who are all teaching me so much. I think of Matthew, who is so enthusiastic about his family, studying, singing, and acting. Celeste, in her quiet way, has taught me that her love for her late husband lives on in her life. The depth of her sorrow and her willingness to move on without denying the person she loved makes me feel OK inside about still loving my mother. There are these sisters, Ruby and Jane, who go home every weekend and sometimes invite some of us from the dorm over for a cookout. Becky will always give me a ride anywhere I need to go, although I am careful not to take advantage of her. My friend Vicki drives this really neat golden-orange car called a Cougar. She introduces me to music that is hard on my ears, but I try to be open-minded. Brian is another friend who tells me that for the first time he has found people who want the same things out of life that he does. His parents often have some of us over to their house. Julie is an English major who has four older sisters. She often proofreads my papers, because my mind moves faster than my pen and I often leave out words. There are so many wonderful kinds of people here, and they all seem to like and accept me, even if I'm not quite up to where they are as human beings.

Sometimes, though, I must appear very foolish to my classmates. Today I smell smoke in the dorm. Being the good Samaritan that I am, I hastily start trying to evacuate people from the building. A friend pulls me into a room and asks what I'm doing. I say, "Don't you smell that fire? It's like burning leaves." She tells me there is no fire, but that some kids are smoking joints. At my uncomprehending look, she explains how people roll marijuana into cigarettes and smoke it to get high. I'm not completely naïve about this; I heard people talking about drugs in high school, but that was always about pills. I didn't know there were drugs that people smoked.

My friends take me to see the people who are smoking the joints. I warn them that the smell is all over the dorm, so they open the windows and put out their cigarettes. I notice they are moving more slowly than usual and my friend says that's because they're a bit stoned. She says that being stoned makes them feel good and that they lose their sense of self-control. I decide I will stay away from these funny-smelling cigarettes. I need to be in control of my life. And I worry that everything I have worked so hard to achieve would be taken away from me if I were caught with this stuff.

Money is becoming an increasing problem. I never knew how important it was before. I truly thought my $1200 would be plenty to see me through college, but it is dwindling fast. After shopping for female clothes and paying a little extra for a private room, I am down to $600. I do participate in the college work study program by cleaning the music hall, but that money goes toward my tuition.

I decide to apply for a job at a supermarket that's within walking distance of the campus. I am nervous about the interview, but all the manager is concerned about is that I show up on time and be nice to customers. He hires me to work from late afternoon until closing time. This will help my financial situation, but another problem is on the horizon. Thanksgiving is coming, and the dorm will be shut down over break. I don't have anywhere to stay. I ask the college administrators if I can't pay extra to stay in my room, but they say no, the entire college closes down for all holidays. "Surely someone will take you in for the holidays," one administrator tells me. Only I know how hurtful those words are.

I've never made a phone call before. I don't tell my dorm friend that. I just tell her I'm not sure how to make a long-distance call, and she shows me. I can't think of anything to do but call Dad, even though his family hates me. After all, since Trevor is living with him until he finishes high school, maybe it won't be so bad if I visit him.

Dad answers the phone. I ask him how Trevor is doing. He says he kicked Trevor out because he was interfering with him and his mother over Alice. He gives me Trevor's phone number. When I ask about Thanksgiving, he tells me to wait a minute and puts the phone down. I can't hear what is being said, but when he comes back he says that his new wife, Gladys, wants to talk to me.

Gladys's voice comes over the line. "You must be incredibly stupid," she says. "After all these years, don't you understand? Get it through your thick head that you and your brothers are not part of this family. We've just managed to get rid of Trevor, and now you start calling. Your dad was stupid enough to adopt you when your mother was alive, but that ended when she died. I don't want any of you four to ever bother us again. Do I make myself clear? You're eighteen years old. Leave this poor man alone, and stay out of our lives!"

I don't get a chance to say anything before she slams the phone down. I just stare at the phone in my hand, overcome with shame and embarrassment. After all these years, I'd let those people get to me again and make me feel like a failure.

Well, this is it. I have to finally accept the fact that the Daddy of my childhood never really existed. I don't have a dad, not even a poor excuse for one.

Right now, I have to put away the pain I am feeling and concentrate on my immediate problem: a place to stay. I go to check out one hotel, but it is filled with people who act like they are drunk. One lady, wearing a short, flashy dress, tells me it is not the right place for a kid like me. But then a classmate, Sam, hears through the grapevine that I'm looking for a hotel. He tells me that he cleans offices in a building called the Berkshire Towers, and that they rent rooms by the week or month. He could use help cleaning, and I could both stay there and make some extra money. I gratefully take him up on his offer. It's good to notice that when one door closes in my life, another one sometimes swings open.

Working at the grocery store and cleaning with Sam keeps me busy. It costs me almost $200 over Thanksgiving to rent a room, go out for meals, and pay for transportation. Also, after someone made a comment about my shoes, I bought a pair of loafers. Everything costs so much. When I arrived at college I had no idea that I'd need to provide my own sheets, towels, pillows, hangers, and a thousand other things that people need. I spent my first night at school sleeping on a bare mattress. The next day I asked Becky to drop me off at a local K-Mart, where I bought what I needed. It's just that when I get done paying for the things that will make me normal I have very little left. In order to keep on top of my expenses and prepare for Christmas, spring break, and the summer months, I need to work more.

Today I call Trevor from the pay phone in the dorm. I ask him how he is, and he says he's having a hard time making ends meet. He says Grandma Resuba got mad at him when he told her Alice was sneaking out with older boys. He thought that at thirteen, she was too young to be dating. He has a small apartment, is working part-time, and is signed up to join the Navy as soon as he graduates. I tell him that I'll come visit him and give him some money. I also tell him an idea that I have had. I remember that my mother used to work at a shirt factory in Seymour, Indiana.

I've learned that we children should have been able to get some social security benefits after she died, but as far as I know, no one ever applied. I am going to take a bus to Seymour and try to find Mother's social security number, so we can get some benefits. Trevor gives me the address of some relatives there he says I can stay with.

I begin my journey, stopping off at the Scranton Greyhound station to meet Trevor. I give him $80, which will cover his rent for two months. It's been almost a year since I have seen him. Looking at him, seventeen years old and taller than I am, I think of the little seven year old crying as he was forced to walk half a block in his underwear for the crime of wetting the bed. That was the first time I knew what real anger was.

I love Trevor; he can be sweet and funny. I promise him that for the next couple of months, I will send him money when I can. He tells me that Tyler is in a reform school for stealing some stuff from a store. Billy has joined the Coast Guard. Trevor says he will be fine, and that it doesn't matter that Dad's family despises us. He says he's his mother's son, and that's all that counts. We hug each other tightly, knowing it may be years before we meet again. As I take my window seat on the bus and wave to him, I ache for the loss of a closeness that we could have had, but now never will.

As I travel towards Seymour, Indiana, I feel

both excitement and fear at the idea that I'll be in a town that once embraced my mother. When I arrive, I go to the shirt factory where she worked. To my amazement, they do have her social security number on file and give it to me. Since I am in town, I decide to go to the library and look up the newspaper articles on my mother's death. "Mother of Five Dies in Trailer Fire," reads the headline. It tells how the fire broke out at 3 a.m., and how my mother's body was found lying at the foot of a bed. Apparently the police thought we children might be in the trailer as well, and they searched for our bodies until someone told them we were at my grandmother's house.

From the newspaper office, I make my way to the local funeral home. The director is there, and I ask him to tell me about my mother's funeral. He remembers it well, he says, because we children were running around playing cowboys and Indians. He says we were too young to realize what had happened. He gives me a copy of her death certificate, which lists the cause of death as smoke inhalation. I ask him if there was any way she could have survived. If I had gone back to the trailer with her that day, might I have been able to save her? He says no; once the furnace exploded, the smoke filled the trailer so quickly that she had no chance. If I had been there I surely would have died too, and even more quickly, as the kids' bedrooms were closer to the furnace than hers.

I hope she didn't feel pain that night.

I find the house of my mother's cousin, and he and his family welcome me for the night. They're nice, but it hurts me once again to see the stark difference between how their children live and how my brothers and I were treated. They tell me they knew nothing about what happened to us after Mother's death; when they asked, they were told we were doing fine with our Dad in Scranton. Although I don't know these people, something within me makes me want them to embrace me and make all my pain go away. As much as I don't want to be, I am still an eight-year-old girl inside.

Back in Pennsylvania, I begin battling with the Social Security Administration. I have applied for benefits for Trevor, Tyler, Alice, and me. I spent some time on the bus agonizing over whether to include Alice. It's not her fault, but her father should have applied for benefits for all of us more than ten years ago, but he didn't. It was he who should have given me my mother's social security number, but he didn't. And Alice will inherit everything from her grandparents. But in all fairness, Alice is our mother's daughter too, and it is only right that she receive her share of benefits. In a way, this pleases me. Grandma Resuba always said that Alice was the daughter she never had. Well, maybe at least with my mother's social security benefits, Alice will remember who her real mother is.

Despite the fact that we could have been collecting benefits all these ten years, the Social Security Administration refuses to make our benefits retroactive to that date. They say it's their policy only to go back one year prior to the date of application. I explain that Dad neglected to apply for the benefits, and that we were only little kids at the time with no one to help us. Their answer is the same: Sorry, no. I can't believe the injustice of this. I write to the president of the United States and our Pennsylvania senator, explaining what has happened. But their responses are the same: it was the responsibility of the adults in our lives, from Dad to our social workers, to apply for benefits on our behalf. As disappointed as I am, I have to satisfy myself with knowing that at least now my brothers and I will get a few of the benefits we should have been receiving all these years, no thanks to the "adults" in our lives.

Tonight as I am working at the grocery store, three men come in just before closing time. I notice them because I am almost ready to close out my drawer and turn the money over to my boss. Suddenly they appear from the back of the store with guns in their hands. Their faces are covered with ski masks, and they are screaming for everyone to get down on the floor. One of the men rushes up behind me, and I feel the barrel of his gun, like a frozen stick, nudging the back of my neck. He orders me to empty the three cash registers into the sack he is holding. I empty two of them, but I know the third is broken and empty. We never use it. I start to tell him this, but he screams, "Do you want me to use this, girlie?" and waves the gun in my face. I hear my boss's voice shouting that I am telling the truth. "That register's been broken for more than a year." They seem to believe him, and turn and run into the night, clutching their bag of money.

I am frozen with terror for many long minutes while my boss calls my name, telling me to snap out of it. He and I spend the next four hours at the police station. I tell him I won't be coming back to the supermarket; I can't work in a place where I might die before accomplishing my goals.

The terror of the experience stays with me for a long time. One odd effect is that I don't get my period again for three months. In a panic, I wonder if I am pregnant. I don't talk to anyone about this, because how can I begin to explain the confusion I feel about everything related to the body and being a woman? The period eventually returns. I wonder if the profound stress of the robbery made it stop.

At school I'm generally on track, but there are many times I don't understand things in my personal life. I constantly work to keep my worlds integrated and under control, but then when something like the robbery comes along, it shatters the illusion that I'm in control of anything at all. I feel just as frightened and helpless as I did as a child. I wish there was someone I felt able to talk to openly about my confusion over things such as the period and whether I could have been pregnant. Even though I don't feel the confidence to do that, I am surrounded by people I consider good role models. There is a history professor who is very nurturing; I have to be careful not to let her know how much I still crave such nurturing. A math teacher is laid-back and makes complicated mathematical concepts easy to understand. My fellow students are of all ages, races, and backgrounds. I am fascinated to hear all of their stories, and realize that for all our differences, we share many of the same goals.

My favorite place to hang out at school is the library. I am comfortable surrounded by books and all those stories of adventures others have lived. An added bonus is the presence of the new librarian, Lois. She is extremely helpful and has a happy, bubbly personality. She's always recommending something new for me to read. One evening, she begins asking me about myself. She has noticed that while I seem open to discussing anything from existential philosophy to the pros and cons of a congressional decision, I never refer to my own past. She's even asked some other people about me, and they all tell her the same: I never mention my life before Alvernia College. She's curious, and asks me if I'm OK.

I like Lois a lot. We have great intellectual conversations, and I can tell she thinks I'm all right. I don't want to jeopardize her opinion about me by telling her too much. I'm afraid that she'll think I'm trying to get attention, or else that she won't like me anymore because I'm so strange.

And so I just tell her that my mother died when I was eight, and that our adoptive father didn't want us.

But Lois doesn't leave it at that. She asks what happened next. I tell her how Dad kept his biological daughter, but put the rest of us in an orphanage on Christmas Eve.

Instead of being disgusted by me, Lois seems fascinated. I tell her a little about the craziness that is foster care. I explain that I keep my past to myself because I know the way I grew up has made me different than other people. Instead of drawing attention to those differences, I just want to try my best to seem normal. My fellow students at Alvernia College have accepted me, and I don't want to risk them withdrawing their friendship.

Instead of pulling away from me, Lois tells me I should tell more of my story. She's astute enough to realize I have only shared with her the tip of the iceberg of my life. She even says I should consider writing a book. Maybe I'll do that. If someone like Lois thinks I'm OK, maybe other people would too.

I have set a new goal for myself: I want to learn to drive. Some of my friends chuckle at my approach to this task: I dip into my savings and buy an old station wagon (which I name Bernadette, after my favorite saint), then try to figure out how to drive it. A classmate of mine, Maxwell, offers to give me driving lessons. He takes me to a big parking lot and shows me how to back up, turn, park, and drive safely. Learning to parallel park is a real challenge, but I eventually pass my driver's test. I am so grateful that I have friends like Maxwell who are willing to teach me things I need in order to move closer to a normal life. The driving lessons become symbolic to me of learning to go places with the help of others.

My success in learning to drive inspires me to accomplish another goal. Long ago, I vowed to change my name. I no longer want to drag around the name of Dad's family, a family that hated and rejected us. I get a copy of my birth certificate and call a lawyer I found in the phone book. When I tell him a little of my story and why I want to change my name, he offers to take the job for a very small fee. He tells me there shouldn't be any problem, but that he will be required to put a notice in the local newspapers in Reading and Scranton to prove to the court that I'm not trying to commit some sort of fraud. I'm not worried that anyone will turn up saying I owe them any money, but the eight-year-old part of me is afraid that Dad's family will see it and write to the judge to tell him that I'll always be a bastard, even if I change my name.

The judge is really nice on the day I go to court. I sit in the witness chair, high off the floor, just like on a TV show. He asks me why I want to change my name. I tell him how my mother died and how Daddy's family hated and abused us. I tell him that if I ever do anything good, I don't want Daddy's family to take credit.

He asks me if I have a name picked out. I say I like the name "Kennedy," because I know the Kennedys have adopted children and kept them. He chuckles at this, then suggests that I take back "Sueck," the name on my birth certificate. I say that is fine with me. With a bang of his gavel he says the change is official, and he wishes me luck in my life.

I am nearly two-thirds done with college.

I've decided to go on to Catholic University in Washington, D.C., for my master's degree in history. I think my fascination with academic history is due in part to the fact that I don't have much of a family history. What I will do after graduate school is still up in the air. I find myself thinking more about becoming a nun. The life of a nun, unmarried and childless and devoted to doing good, would suit the goals I've set on my various "survival lists." So far, I don't feel that I've made much of a difference with my life. As a nun, maybe I could become totally focused on the needs of others, without a thought for myself.

Today is my twenty-first birthday; next month I will be a senior in college. By all the official standards I am now an adult, entitled to the same rights as every other adult I encounter. If only turning twenty-one could make me feel emotionally grown up! For me, the only difference is that I can now legally drink, but I won't because of all the alcoholic orphans that I've met. The question for me from here on out is, "Now what?"

Graduate school continues to seem like the right next step. I take the Graduate Record Exam, the test required to get into grad school. Like the SAT, it gives me a headache, but I do all right, and my application to Catholic University is accepted. I am happy at this further evidence that I'm at least book-smart.

It is time for my college graduation. In my heart I ask my mother if she can believe that her little girl has accomplished such a goal. From the moment I stepped off that Greyhound bus four years ago, I have enjoyed my time at Alvernia. While I've been academically challenged, I've also been warmly embraced by people who have taught me far more than I ever expected to learn. Instead of the temporary friends of high school, here I have made real friends. I truly feel that this is the best little college in America.

The college gives us each seven tickets so our family and friends can attend our graduation. I give mine away because I have no family to invite. The only friends I have are here at Alvernia, and they will already be attending the ceremony. I try not to think about the fact that no one from my past is here to see what I have accomplished. I feel both a sense of sweet revenge on those people who said I would never amount to anything, and a sense of sadness that no one here knows where I came from and what I have overcome. But mostly I feel simply joy that I am standing here as a college graduate.

In no time, it seems, I am plunged into my life as a graduate student in Washington, D.C. I'm studying history and religion, so I could possibly teach or go on to law school. I'm working two jobs to pay for school as I go along. One of my jobs is in the law library. It is a really cool place, and I've learned a lot about how to do legal research. The thing that discourages me from considering law as a profession is that the women lawyers look so stylish and professional. They have a confidence and air of certainty that I certainly lack. I can't imagine ever fitting in with them. As my two years of graduate school come to a close, I decide that joining a convent and becoming a nun is what God wants for my life. I've spent a lot of time in prayer over this decision. I have always wanted to live my life for a noble purpose, and becoming a nun seems like a wonderful expression of my love for God and the love I know He has always had for me. I also like the idea that a nun doesn't need a past; that she changes her name and takes the other nuns in her convent as her family. I try to keep these reasons in the back of my mind, however, because they seem less worthy than my desire to serve God and humanity.

Today an incident occurred that nearly stopped my heart with shock. When I came home from work, I found a note on my dorm door. It gave the name and number of a social worker and had this message: "Jerri. Call this person right away. Your mother has been found alive and well."

As insane as it was, my eight-year-old's heart

nearly burst with joy as I raced for the pay phone and dialed the social worker's number. As I gushed my relief and happiness into the phone, exclaiming how I had known all those years ago Mother hadn't really died, the social worker sounded more and more confused. Finally she broke in, asking me for my full name. In a gentle voice, she explained that there had been a mistake. The person the note had been intended for was another woman named Jerri, who worked over in the maintenance department. Her mother had Alzheimer's disease and had become lost over the weekend. The social worker apologized again for getting my hopes up.

Embarrassed, I thanked her and hung up. I thought to myself that there must be something truly wrong with me. At the age of twenty-three, how could I still be capable of believing something so impossible? Will my orphaned child's heart ever get into step with my adult mind and body?

Graduation day comes, and I receive my master's degree. My graduation from Catholic University is very different from my college graduation. I use my tickets to invite friends from Alvernia to witness the occasion. It makes me feel good that there are people willing to travel to be with me today.

I have the summer to prepare to enter the convent. I still think it's the best thing to do, although I can't shake off some doubts. Is this decision God's will, or my will? Should I listen to friends who suggest that I am running away from life, looking for a safe place to hide? I know that I can make it in the outside world in a material, financial sense. But I also know that despite all my accomplishments in the past few years, I am still afraid of people and of living in a "normal" world that still feels alien to me. I know that part of the pull of the convent is that it will provide structure and a sense of belonging, even if it is on an institutional and not a personal level. I also fear the anger I know I am capable of—the anger I still feel over Mother leaving us, and the anger at Daddy's family that even now can almost consume me if I allow myself to think of them. As a nun, I believe that I will be living the right kind of life, one that won't allow me to be angry about things I cannot change.

$\mathscr{T}$HE CONVENT YEARS

AGES 24 *to* 34

$\mathscr{D}$ear Mother,

I have begun what I believe will be a good way of life. Since I cannot imagine that I will live longer than you did, I am convinced I will die by the time I am thirty-one. It is best that I use the time left to me to serve humanity. I know God has always loved me, and this seems like an appropriate "thank-you" to Him.

This way of life suits me in many ways. My past is non-essential here. I am accepted as part of the group. I have found a way to live without being noticed.

The only thing I don't like is this vow of obedience. As a nun, I have to take three vows: poverty, chastity, and obedience. The first two are no problem. I have always been poor, and I don't plan to sleep with anyone. But obedience is tough, and this is why: My first assignment is to teach eighth grade near Scranton, the city that I was determined never to return to. When I ask to be sent somewhere—anywhere—else for personal reasons, I am told that it is God's will that I go there. I am also reminded that nothing that happened before I entered the convent matters.

I dread going out on this assignment. I will do the best I can, and hope that my superior is right about the past being irrelevant.

God, can doing Your will change what I know to be true? How can anyone know for sure what is Your will?

Love,
Jerri

One of the things that I like about being a nun is that I'm not expected to have a past. Constant change and non-attachment are the norm, and every year I am sent to teach at a different school. Here at my first assignment, I am living with a group of eleven nuns. I can't help but notice that there is an enormous difference in our ages. The others are in their sixties at the very least, and some are much older.

My life is incredibly busy, especially since I am the only one of the eleven who drives. I am constantly on call. Along with teaching and the prayer schedule, there is a constant round of hospital visits, wakes, and funerals to attend. I haven't been to a funeral since my mother's, and I've never attended a viewing before. I find them very difficult. Sometimes I can't take my eyes off the dead, especially their hands, as I try to comprehend the magnitude of death. I marvel at the delicacy and fragility of our lives.

The only personal problem I'm dealing with is being so close to Scranton. Try as I might, when I go out in public I still feel like the bastard child I try to forget ever existed. I'm always expecting to run into Dad's family and hear them say that I am nothing and no one. After earning two degrees and making over my life, I still fear them so. I walk around with my head down so I won't see them if they're nearby. At night, I am tortured with intense, raging dreams about them. Apparently even working in God's name doesn't erase those human elements of fear, shame, and self-loathing.

Today is the ceremony in which I choose a new name to represent my new life. This will be my fourth name in twenty-five years. But this is different; this will be a name for a totally new person. Nothing that happened in the past will be part of this person's reality.

I choose the name Bernadette Marie. Bernadette was a saint who had a hard life. She had a vision of Jesus' mother appearing to her, and in the beginning not even the church believed her. Thank God I never had a vision. When I was a child I used to pray that everyone would stay in heaven and not appear to me. My life was chaotic enough; I didn't need to try to explain a miracle. I picked the name Marie in honor of Jesus' mother, and besides, I liked the way the name sounded when I said it: Sister Bernadette Marie.

So I have gone from being Jerri Diane Sueck to Jerri Diane Zigga, back to Jerri Diane

Sueck again, and now Sister Bernadette Marie. Not a bad track record.

Life at the convent is a blur of activity, one that leaves little time for the darkness to creep in, except when I am forced to sleep and am wracked by dreams of the past. One of the most rewarding experiences I've had involved a young boy at school. Leo's father died around Christmas, and it was clear the boy had been very attached to him. Several months later, I asked Leo to do an assignment. He snapped "No!," which was very unlike him. Instead of scolding him, I took him to the library where we could be alone. Looking him in the face, I said, "You miss him, don't you?"

Leo started crying. He said that no one understands how much he missed his Dad, and how it was getting harder to live without him instead of easier. He said I could never understand how much it hurt, and how he begs God to send his father back.

My determination to keep my past private flew out the window. I told Leo just a little, about how I'd lost my mother at a very young age, and the terrible aching and loneliness I had experienced. Leo's eyes grew wide; he seemed so relieved. "You don't think I'm crazy to feel this way?" he said. I told him absolutely not, and that he needed to confide in his mother and let her know how much he was hurting. I also asked him to let other people nurture him, telling him that accepting their love and comfort was in no way a betrayal of his father. "You'll always miss your father, even when you're a grown man," I told him. "But that's how we honor those we've loved; by keeping them alive in our hearts." I gently told Leo that it was possible his mother would remarry some day, and that that, too, could be a good thing. God never meant for any child to remain fatherless or motherless.

Later, I called Leo's mother and let her know about our talk. She was grateful, saying that her son had been becoming more withdrawn and that she hadn't been sure how to help him. I reminded her that the death of his father didn't mean that Leo didn't need fathering, and I encouraged her to provide other father figures in his life. She said she had an older son, in his twenties, and she would talk to him about taking his younger brother under his wing.

I'm glad to have done something that might help Leo find the nurturing he needs so badly now. I wish I could do the same for every orphaned child. In the religion class I teach, there are two children whose parents have died. One of them lost both parents to drug overdoses. Because they weren't employed, there was no social security or life insurance, and no family to take her in. She is a ward of the state and lives in a group home with five other girls. She is a really nice person, and a fair student.

The other girl's mother died in a car accident, and her father, a police officer, died in the line of duty. Her parents had made a will, naming guardians for her in case anything happened to them, and those people had taken her in. There was social security, life insurance, and benefits from her father's work as a policeman.

I think the more fortunate orphan deserves all of this aid, and as much emotional support as she can get. I only wish that the unlucky orphan had the same. It seems to me that when a child is born, its parents should be required to make a will, writing down a plan for someone to care for that child if they can't do it. I think life insurance should be mandatory, with the children as beneficiaries. Planning like this could go a long way towards bridging the gap between the lucky and the unlucky orphan. The way it is now, even in death there are haves and have-nots.

Well, I am thirty-one years old now. Somehow I was sure I would not outlive my mother, but here I am. This throws me into a state of confusion. I had my life planned around dying by this age. Now what do I do? I don't regret the choices I've made that have brought me here, but I wonder if it's time to set some new goals. The school that I am assigned to this year is a marvelous place of life and excitement. It is located in the middle of a struggling Philadelphia neighborhood, and it has a wonderful name: Little Flower High School. It is named in honor of St. Theresa, who was called the "little flower" because she tried not to draw attention to herself as she served God. The school serves working-class families who are trying to show their daughters a moral path in life. The thing that strikes me is the spirit that resonates throughout the hallway and anywhere the girls gather. The electricity just crackles. There's a wonderful sense of community as well; very few kids are left to themselves to become loners. Discipline is tight, but everyone is so supportive. I love absorbing the energy from the staff and from the girls who are always willing to do interesting projects.

One of my favorite projects is "Operation Santa Claus." At Christmas, each religion class is assigned a family. The class is responsible for providing that family with food and presents. As a religion teacher, I am involved with five families, and I feel personally responsible for every one of them. I love knowing that we will provide them with what my brothers and I were denied.

Today was a momentous day. I met the first human being who I believe glimpses the real truth about me, but doesn't think I am crazy.

Her name is Sister Leah, and she is from another community of nuns. She is a counselor by training, and when I start to talk to her, she begins asking me some relevant questions. Instead of encouraging me to put the past behind me and move on, she shocks me by saying she believes I have some serious issues to come to terms with. She actually says that my efforts to forget the past are doing more harm than good. She is aghast at the way I was shuffled from place to place after my mother's death, and tells me that I must be very strong not to have completely broken down mentally under that kind of pressure. She encourages me to go into therapy, saying that by refusing to come to terms with my extraordinary past is to cheat myself out of life as a whole person.

My conversation with Leah is a tremendous relief to me. Finally someone has told me what I have always known to be true: that the shattering experiences of my young life cannot and should not be swept under the carpet and forgotten. If I am ever to feel like a whole human being, not afraid of myself and of others, I need to make some changes. I agree that I need to find a therapist. Leah offers to meet with me for counseling until I can find someone permanent.

But when I approach the charge person to ask permission to get counseling, she is taken aback by my request. "People who go into counseling leave the convent," she states. "God should be enough support for you." I explain that I don't want to leave the convent; I just need to sort out some issues surrounding my mother's death. "Why are you focusing on the past?" she asks. "Your energy should be invested in serving God, through your service to others."

I try to reassure her that this isn't about doubting God, but I feel like I'm asking her for the moon. Finally, she gives me reluctant permission to meet with Leah, but reminds me that she expects me to make rapid progress. Her parting shot is this: "Remember, whatever problems you have, you brought here. We're not responsible for anything."

I tell myself she doesn't have to worry about my blaming the nuns for anything. I've long ago learned to blame myself for everything wrong in my life.

For a couple of months, I have counseling sessions with Leah. The psychological tests I take diagnose me as suffering from post-traumatic stress syndrome—the same sort of syndrome that soldiers sometimes experience after returning from war. While my talks with Leah are helpful, it's very difficult to make much progress with so little support. I am repeatedly told that I am wrong to focus on the past; that Jesus should be enough help for me; that I should be stronger than this. I remind myself that even Jesus surrounded himself with advisors and friends. I figure that if Jesus needed a support group, I am in good company.

Another problem is that the charge person is requesting access to all my records, including what goes on in my sessions with Leah.

Finally, I ask to see the superior charge person—someone further up the ladder of authority in our province. I tell her the situation and ask for a leave of absence for health reasons. Away from the convent, I figure I can work freely with a therapist and then return when I am feeling healthier. She turns down my request for a leave of absence, but tells me not to worry about the charge person gaining access to my records. She also offers to give me use of a car for my meetings with Leah.

Feeling encouraged, I go back to my life at the convent, and things go all right for a couple of months. But then I get a furious phone call from the charge person, berating me for going over her head and talking to her superior. I tell her again how vulnerable and intimidated she makes me feel, especially with her demand for the records of my counseling sessions, but that doesn't calm her down. She reminds me again that as the supervisor of the community, she is entitled to see my information.

Later, I call the superior charge person. She says she can't help me; that she has to be concerned about all the sisters in general, not one in particular. I have nothing to say, so I just hang up.

A few days later, I get a letter from the charge person terminating my assignment at Little Flower High School. I have been reassigned to teach eighth grade in Scranton. When I call her to ask if there is anything I can say to change her mind, she says no. If I wish to remain with the order, returning to Scranton is my only choice.

Tonight as I lie in bed trying to figure out what to do, I realize that it is the denial of my past that has brought me to this painful point. There is no way I can continue being a nun if I cannot understand and accept my own humanity. I know that leaving the convent will not solve my problems, any more than entering it did. I must seek out the help of other people as I confront the demons of my past. The chapter of my life as a nun is over.

$\mathcal{M}$Y EMERGENCE INTO LIFE

AGE 34 *to* PRESENT

$\mathcal{D}$ear Mother,

Today I am thirty-three years old and have left the convent. I live in a small two-bedroom apartment here in Philadelphia. I'm sharing it with a roommate, a woman I met while teaching at Little Flower High School. She is engaged to a nice guy.

The first thing I do after getting my own place is adopt a kitten I call Molly. I've always wanted a pet, something I can cuddle and feel responsible for. I also want to allow myself to become attached to a living creature. With all the damage inside me, I don't know if I can manage that with a human being, so I will start with Molly. If I can feel a bond with a cat, then maybe I can move on to a dog and eventually people.

I have no money, so I've taken three jobs. During the day, I substitute teach at a local high school. At night I work on a psychiatric unit at a state hospital, and on the weekends I care for some elderly clients. I need the money, but I also work so much in order to stay awake as much as possible. My night terrors and dreams continue to haunt me.

I know I need to find a way out of the self-imposed isolation that I'm living in now. I need to start looking for a counselor who can help me put back together what was blown apart so long ago. If I am ever going to live in the real world, as opposed to educational or religious institutions, I need to accept who and what I am and make the best of whatever truths I discover. Denying who and what I am is no longer working for me. I have to believe that deep down inside there is a human being worth salvaging. I can't keep running from myself. I must find a way to bring all the splintered parts of me together.

Love,
Jerri

I am finding life in the adult world to be very stressful. I obviously missed out on some important lessons growing up. Managing my time and my money is an overwhelming task. I don't know how to say "no" when people request either. Three times now I have sold an old car, handing over the title before any payments were made. Three times I haven't gotten my money. I "sold" a brand-new air conditioner—only the buyer never paid me for it. I have to learn not to let people take advantage of me.

I realize I have lived most of my life within the structure of an institution. I managed to do well in school because it had rules and schedules that I understood. Stepping from that world into teaching and the convent seemed like a natural, continuing flow. But now I'm facing the demands of ordinary daily life. I feel like I'm in a fog sometimes, trying to learn the language of the ordinary world.

I begin to feel a little more settled when I am hired as a full-time high school teacher here in Philadelphia. I actually manage to find a therapist who I feel comfortable with, and talking with her has been a big help and a relief. She confirms my realization that trying to forget about my past is an impossible task. It's part of who I am, and I have to deal with it.

My life starts to look more normal when I cut back my hours at the hospital, and stop taking care of all but one of my elderly clients. I keep one old lady because she is so mean and nasty that no one else is willing to deal with her. Maybe it's Catholic guilt, but I end up feeling responsible for her. She has her nice moments, but she often feels lonely and abandoned. Her son visits her, but she wants someone with her all the time and she complains an awful lot. I hope if I live as long as she does that I will be gracious to the people who care for me.

I'm teaching junior and senior history classes at a large high school called Franklin Learning Center. There's a nice sense of camaraderie here, and most of us enjoy each other's company. As usual, I find the assortment of characters around me fascinating. My principal is a very formal person with a dry sense of humor. The vice-principal reminds me of those Energizer Bunny commercials—she's got energy that just won't quit. One teacher makes me laugh by assigning nicknames to other teachers: there's "Queen of Ma Bell" and "Queen of the IBM Lab." Every kid has his or her own style. One comes to see me every morning because he's determined to go to college and wants to make sure he's doing everything right. Another talks to me about her dreams of a career in Hollywood. I encourage them to believe in their dreams, telling them that if they're willing to pay the dues, they can aspire to anything.

Occasionally I run into a student who needs something more personal from me. One of my boys, Fred, has talked to me on nearly a daily basis since I learned, just by chance, that his mother died in a plane crash during his freshman year. I told him that I'd lost my mother, too, and he seemed relieved to know I understood the depth of his sadness. When I asked Fred what he missed most about his mom, he told me how he used to sit at the dining table doing his homework. When his mom would walk by, she would tousle his hair or grab him in a bear hug, telling him what a great kid he was. I told Fred I know how important those mother touches are, and tears come to his eyes. He tells me how his sister cried the night before her prom, and how he has a constant sense of something missing from his life.

Fred and I have talked many times during his high school years. He thanks me for listening and says that after his mom died, he wanted to die, too. Now he intends to live in a way that will honor everything she has taught him, dreamed for him, and sacrificed for him. I love Fred for his honesty and willingness to try to understand the cards that life has dealt him.

It comforts me to think that through my experience, I may have learned things that are of help to others. At the psych hospital where I work part time, I have gotten to know Mark, a very nice man. He is married to a beautiful woman and they have two little girls. When we talk about my past, he says it's a wonder that I'm not a psychiatric patient myself.

Recently Mark went to the doctor after his knee buckled under him as he held his baby daughter. He was diagnosed with multiple sclerosis—MS. He will have to learn to live with what can be a devastating disease. When I asked Mark how he was doing, he said he remembered me saying that as an orphan, I just do the best I can and look for those people or things that can make up for what I have lost. Mark says that is his attitude, too. He considers himself very lucky because the disease is affecting only his legs. With his arms he can hold his daughters and hug his wife and work on his computer. And he has a supportive family that he knows will always be there for him. Mark continues to be as good-humored and gracious a person as he was before he learned he had MS.

One of those sucker-punches that life sometimes throws hits me today. I return from work to find a message on my answering machine. It is from my mother's youngest sister, in Indiana. She has left her number and wants me to call her.

Apparently Billy has given her my unlisted phone number. I knew he'd been in touch with them occasionally. Although I have not seen Billy since I was ten years old, I talk to him every now and then. He is married and living in Alaska. He tells me he holds only Daddy's family responsible for our abuse and neglect.

I debate within myself for a week before calling Indiana. When I do call, my aunt answers the phone as if the past thirty-two years have never happened. But as she says, "Oh, how have you been?" I cut her off with the question, "Did my mother love me?" There is silence at the other end, and then she answers that my mother loved all her children deeply.

She wants me to come for a visit. I tell her I don't know what to say to that, because they have been dead to me for so long. She says that my grandmother is nearly eighty years old, and that she often cries because of all my mother's children, I am the only one who has never been in touch.

I remind this aunt that my grandmother was only forty-seven when she said "no" to taking us. I remind her that she and her sister were in their twenties when my mother died. Why should I go visit people who cared so little for our well-being?

My aunt tells me I need to understand the circumstances at the time. My grandmother had her hands full with her own husband, and she and her sister had young children to worry about. At the time, she says, her own life was in turmoil due to a divorce and remarriage.

"Turmoil?" I ask her. "Try living like my brothers and I lived. Then talk to me about turmoil."

She says I should be more like my brothers and realize that for our grandmother's sake, I should come and give her peace before she dies. She adds that she would take me to see my mother's grave. "Your mother would have forgiven us, and you should be able to forgive us, too," she adds.

She goes on to say how my mother's death devastated the family. "Maybe it's just me," I reply, "but I can't imagine having a daughter or sister dying, leaving four orphaned children, and never bothering to check on them." She tells me that adult life is complicated, and that sometimes timing is just off. She asks again if I will come visit. I say I will think about it.

After I hang up, all I can do is wonder, where was this aunt when I was eight, or ten, or twelve years old?

I find it interesting that despite their ability to forgive my mother's family, none of my brothers have returned to live in Indiana. I am also curious about my mother's relationship with her family. If they were as upset by her death as they say they were, why didn't they seek us out in our time of need? The more I think about it, the odder this seems. After all, it wasn't us kids that they knew well; it was she. She had bonded with them, she knew their stories. She shared their family culture and history. Something does not make sense here.

After thinking about it for some time, I decide that I will go to Indiana. I won't deny them whatever peace my visit can give, although I'm still not sure they have a clue about the moral lapse they committed concerning us children. Mostly I look at this journey as a chance to retrace Mother's footsteps in order to learn more about who she was, and what my place was in her world. As I am considering writing a book, I want to stand by my mother's grave and ask her blessing for this venture. In the end, I am going to her family for her sake. She broke bread with my grandmother on the night before she died. Maybe she'd want me to let the old woman off the hook.

When I arrive in Indiana, I am greeted as though I've been on a sightseeing tour of the world and am now returning in triumph to share my adventures. "Jerri! How nice to see you!" they say, and come at me with hugs and kisses. I am polite, but I can't just play along. I have a frank talk with everyone, explaining how their lack of action contributed to the splintering of my mother's family. The family members that seem to understand me best are my two cousins. They are horrified to learn that their mother and grandmother had abandoned us. I think my mother would have appreciated hearing them say indignantly, "If it'd been me, I never would have come back to Indiana!"

I try to learn more about my mother from her sisters, but they aren't a great deal of help. They were much younger than she and weren't around her that much. They mention that her first cousins in Kentucky grew up with her, and that they knew her best. So I take my grandmother and we drive to Kentucky to see that part of my family. There I learn a family secret—at least a secret to me—that helps, just as little, to explain why my mother's family could have behaved so coldly towards us in our time of need.

It turns out that my grandmother gave birth to my mother when she was only fifteen years old. Because she was so young, my grandmother gave the baby to her own mother to raise. For the first five years of her life, Mother lived with her grandmother. Her best friends and playmates were her first cousins. My grandmother then married and Mother went to live with her real mother and stepfather, but her heart had been split. She always felt more comfortable in her grandmother's home. As I talk with my grandmother, it becomes apparent that even after all these years, she resents my mother's attachment to my great-grandmother. My grandmother speaks with venom of how her mother spoiled my mother for the first five years of her childhood. She also resented my great-grandmother interfering with the way she raised my mother. I get the sense that my great-grandmother was very strict with her own daughter, but that she was more lenient with my mother, even doting on her. It's funny how family secrets have a way of smacking those who were never around for the original event.

With this story, a little light is shed on what had been, to me, the greatest mystery of my childhood. I could never understand how women with normal attachments to their daughter and sister could have been so unconcerned about the welfare of her children. Now I realize that the ordinary family connections I believed were there may not have existed after all. There were undercurrents of jealousy, hostility, and estrangement that I'd never suspected. Although

I still can't understand or accept my Indiana relatives' actions—or lack of actions—I can now forgive them.

I learn some more family news. At nineteen, Alice married a man twenty years older than she. She has four sons. After returning home from my trip to Indiana, I begin to hear from her occasionally. Although she'd had so many more opportunities than Billy, Trevor, Tyler, or me, she is still struggling to get herself together. When she asks me for money, I tell her she needs to go back to school and prepare for a career.

As I've written this book, I realize what a gift it was to have the company of my brothers in those early years. I think Mother would have been so proud of Billy, Trevor, Tyler, and me. Although I haven't seen Billy since that awful Christmas Eve so many years ago, I will never forget the courage of my wonderful big brother. He was just a child himself, but he tried so hard to protect the rest of us. Trevor is happily married and living in Iowa with his wife and four children. Tyler is in Iowa as well, still trying to get his life together. To my surprise, I learn both Trevor and Tyler, like me, have changed their last names. None of my brothers has ever returned to Pennsylvania.

As for me, I am doing well. I've recently bought a little row house in Philadelphia, where I live with my dogs and my cat. It will do until I build the log cabin in the woods that I dream about. Learning to make my house into a home is one of those tasks that I'm still working on. When I first moved in, I was overwhelmed with the sense of being responsible for such a big space. For the first two years, I slept on the couch in the living room, for fear that I'd be trapped by a fire in my bedroom. But gradually I am learning to relax here. I've put some candles on the tables and pictures on the walls, and even planted some flowers in my tiny front yard.

I have surrounded myself with both human and animal friends. My human friends fill so many needs: one reminds me to take my vitamins; another drags me out shopping; many read my writing and give me encouragement as I try to get my story down on paper. My students at the high school where I teach have become my greatest cheerleaders; many of them even cried when I read part of my story for the senior English class. Finding an abandoned beagle lost in a snowstorm led me to become involved in animal rescue work. A loose network of us provides help to our four-legged friends who have been orphaned or abused. Every time I help one of those unfortunate animals find a happy home, I feel like I've healed a tiny bit of myself.

Still, for all the progress I've made, I am constantly aware of the children in the world who are growing up as I did. There are over

580,000 American children in foster care, and almost 200,000 available for adoption. The average length of time a child spends in foster care is eight and a half years. What is most disturbing to me is that nearly seventy percent of foster kids will never finish high school. Only three percent graduate from college. A huge percentage of foster children end up homeless at some point in their lives, and their own children frequently become wards of the state. If any racial or ethnic group claimed statistics like that, the situation would be declared a national emergency. But foster children are a powerless group, almost invisible. There is no one to speak for them. I hope in a small way this story will open the eyes of its readers to the forgotten children all around them.

$\mathcal{D}$ear Mother,

Words can never express the gratitude I feel for the way you've shared my journey through life. I truly believe that making a special place in my heart for you and God allowed me to heal and grow, even as I endured the traumas of life.

When you died, I tried desperately to find you in my childish ways. I asked Daddy's family about you, but you know how that worked out. But I kept talking to you so I wouldn't lose the connection we once shared. Eventually I realized that your spirit was somewhere, listening to my whispered words. That made me so much less lonely, despite all my confusion.

When I was a child, I used to tell Daddy's mother that someday I would tell you everything. Maybe through this book I finally have. This story is for you; for all the mothers who truly mother; and for all the children who have known abandonment.

One of my favorite movies is called Beaches, with Bette Midler. In the end, Bette becomes a mother of the heart to her best friend's orphaned little girl. As Bette takes that child's hand, her voice is heard singing the haunting song, "You are the wind beneath my wings." Those words honestly describe how I feel about you and God, Mother. The two of you have truly been the wind beneath my wings.

Love,
Jerri